When couples hit a rough patch in their marriage, the tendency for most is to seek better ways of behaving and performing in order to improve the relationship. The problem, of course, is that outward behavior doesn't always reflect the true state of our hearts! In their new book, Brad and Marilyn Rhoads have extended a gospel-oriented approach to marriage that is rooted in the kind of love and grace Christ holds out to us.

JIM DALY, President, Focus on the Family

God's grace is freeing and transformative. This book will help you extend that grace to your spouse and set your marriage free to thrive.

BOB GOFF, *New York Times* bestselling author

I have been urging the Rhoads to write this book for fifteen years. Trust me when I say that *The Grace Marriage* is a must-read! This book has been life-tested in Marilyn and Brad's marriage, but also in years of counseling and teaching. Its gospel focus will shape your sense of identity and structure your expectations. It will help you see the trap of a performance-based marriage and the beauty of a grace-based marriage. The authors' self-disclosure in this book will model what it means to be complete in Christ. It is simple and accessible without being shallow. It is profoundly theological and yet eminently practical. May God use this book to transform marriages in the body of Christ to be like a "city on a hill" that cannot be hidden.

TEDD TRIPP, pastor emeritus, author, conference speaker

What a brilliant move to look at every aspect of marriage under the rubric of grace! Grace is lovely and precious; even more, it reflects the beauty of Jesus, which this book does as well. After reading this marvelous book, you will never look at your marriage through the same lens again.

GARY THOMAS, author of *Sacred Marriage* and *Cherish*

In our research, one of the most crucial factors for a great marriage is having grace with your spouse. In this life-giving book, Brad and Marilyn convey deep truths about *how* to do exactly that. Their everyday stories and illustrations will help you connect the truths they share to your own everyday journey with your spouse, no matter where you are in your marriage. We highly recommend that you read *The Grace Marriage*—with your spouse—as it will breathe hope and life into your heart and marriage.

JEFF AND SHAUNTI FELDHAHN, social researchers and bestselling authors of *For Women Only* and *For Men Only*

Brad and Marilyn are a couple that walks the talk. The message of *The Grace Marriage* is not just one they write about, it's one they live. I love their balanced approach of grace and truth, and their message of investing in your marriage will inspire and challenge you to do the same. It takes intentional work to move your marriage to a healthy place, and this book will help give you a practical plan to take those next steps.

DEBRA FILETA, licensed professional counselor and bestselling author

Brad and Marilyn's book is an honest, transparent, deep dive into the realities that married couples face every day. Their discussion transforms the trifecta of communication, money, and sex into a gentle conversation about God's grace. These potentially kryptonite issues can weaken the strongest marriages. Yet the Rhoads tackle each with courage, clarity, and biblically based strategies. I particularly love their reminder that "God uses marriage—and sometimes our spouse, specifically—as an avenue of grace to grow us more into His likeness." This book should be required reading for every marriage ministry and premarital program.

ROD PATTERSON, Executive Leader, International Christian Brotherhood; author of *Guard Your Gates*

I know of no other book that focuses more on living out the gospel in your marriage than this one. Readers with a shallow understanding of the gospel will strengthen not only their marriage, but their grasp of God's saving grace in Christ as well. Those with a clear understanding of it will see its practical implications for marriage as never before. The Rhoads have written this book in an easy-to-read style, amply illustrating their early naiveté about marriage and the resulting failures, along with how they learned to grow in their relationship by intentionally investing in it. I know Brad well. He's humbly transparent about both his failures (especially) and successes in his marriage to Marilyn. But I don't know anyone who prioritizes his marriage more than he does. The Rhoads won't give you the impression in this book that they have achieved marital perfection, but they will show you biblical reasons and real-life (with five kids!) suggestions on how they've dramatically improved their marriage and how you can too.

DONALD S. WHITNEY, Professor of Biblical Spirituality and Associate Dean at The Southern Baptist Theological Seminary (Louisville, KY); author of *Spiritual Disciplines for the Christian Life*, *Praying the Bible*, and *Family Worship*

Brad and Marilyn Rhoads lead with their hearts as they teach us how to experience intentionality in our marriages. Consistently investing in and valuing our spouse is a transforming catalyst in our homes–and only achieved through the power of the gospel. What a valuable framework and guide they equip husbands and wives with!

CARL CATON, President, The Marriage Initiative

If there is one resource every family pastor and Christian marriage and family therapist should have on their shelf, it is *The Grace Marriage*. Brad and Marilyn have done a masterful job weaving personal stories alongside Scripture in order to make the gospel's relevance come alive with regard to marriage. The balance of wisdom, conviction, and tenderness are refreshing.

NATHAN THOMPSON, LPCC, Family Pastor, Southeast Christian Church

This will become *the* book for marriage. It's honest, engaging, and practical. You'll laugh a lot. But most importantly, it absolutely drips the grace and love of Christ.

JAMUS EDWARDS, Pastor for Preaching & Vision, Pleasant Valley Community Church

The Grace Marriage is an excellent book that holds the key to marriage . . . grace. It's the grace of Jesus that lays the firm foundation for everything in marriage. When spouses are intentionally extending grace to one another,

their marriage will flourish and can successfully navigate personality differences, financial challenges, and even marital crises.
HOWARD DAYTON, Founder, Compass – Finances God's Way

Great storytelling. Humor. Strong truth. Practical application. There is perhaps no better way to learn about tough subjects. In *The Grace Marriage*, Brad and Marilyn Rhoads bring together all of these elements to help Christians gain a new perspective and strengthen their marriages. I'm recommending this book everywhere I go!
JOSEPH SANGL, President & CEO, INJOY Stewardship Solutions

When a book tells a fascinating story while exposing the reader to rock-solid doctrine, the heart of Jesus, and a revolutionary strategy for marriage, one can't help but be enthralled. Not only will *The Grace Marriage* transfix you, it will transform your marriage while transforming your heart.
RICK HOWERTON, Pastor of Rockwall Groups, Lakepointe Church; author, *A Different Kind of Tribe: Embracing the New Small-Group Dynamic*

As we listened to the story of their marriage, and how God transformed their marriage, all of us wanted God's grace for our own marriages! Brad and Marilyn point us to the grace of Christ and solid biblical principles that motivate us to "do marriage" God's way. Thank you, Brad and Marilyn, for being transparent and honest with your own struggles and the joy you found in surrendering yourselves to God's grace!
GREG ALLEN, Campus Pastor, Southeast Christian Church

We know that grace saves! In *The Grace Marriage*, the Rhoads help Christians see, in a real-life, practical way, how grace can play the definitive role in fostering healthy, Christ-centered marriages. This book will ignite a fire of renewal in married life across the country.
J.P. DE GANCE, founder and president, Communio

As followers of Christ, the grace offered by our Lord is our salvation and hope. Could this be any less true in our marriages? Certainly not! In this great book, Brad and Marilyn skillfully show us how to receive God's grace, enjoy it fully, and effectively invest it in both our spouse and our relationship. The result is a divinely blessed, grace-filled life *and* marriage. Why settle for less!
ROBERT S. PAUL, Vice President, Focus on the Family Marriage Institute

As I talk to churches around the country, I continue to hear about the impact Brad and Marylin are having on couples. As you read this book, I am sure you will understand why!
JOHN MCGEE, Senior Director, Watermark Resources

Brad and Marilyn have written a fantastic book on marriage that centers around Jesus Christ. From the standpoint of the Word of God, their own experiences, and honest transparency and heart-driven questions, this book offers guidelines for couples to stay connected to each other. The book also addresses the major aspects of marriage through the lens of the gospel. I truly believe that your marriage will be transformed, enriched, and healthy after reading this book.
JON BELL, Campus Pastor (Aurora Campus), Harvest Bible Chapel

I am so excited about *The Grace Marriage* getting into the hands of married couples everywhere. Godly, Christ-honoring marriages are desperately needed in our culture today. I love how this book is rooted in a sound theological framework and applied very practically to every area of marriage. I highly recommend going through this book with your spouse.

AFSHIN ZIAFAT, Lead Pastor, Providence Church (Frisco, TX) and council member for The Gospel Coalition

This is an honest, touching, and real-life meditation on the meaning, methods, and manners of a grace-filled and Christ-focused marriage. By generously sharing their story of courtship, marriage, and parenthood—warts and all—Brad and Marilyn Rhoads teach us that marriage is a lifelong covenant of love and sacrifice, not a utilitarian contract of works and performance. The authors further show how a grace-filled Christian marriage practically and realistically plays out in marital communication, sexual exchange, household finance, children's upbringing, crisis management, and more. Wistful singles, courting couples, married spouses, marital counselors, and Christian pastors alike will benefit from this lovely book.

JOHN WITTE, Faculty Director, Center for the Study of Law and Religion, Emory University

In *The Grace Marriage*, Brad and Marilyn beckon us to the marriage-transforming power of God's grace in all its hope-bringing, pride-killing, Christ-exalting sweetness. This book is theologically rich, well-written, practically oriented, and much-needed today. Read to remember how truly you are known and how fully you are loved. Read also to recognize fresh ways to root your marriage in the gracious soil of the gospel.

NATHAN TARR, Associate Professor of Pastoral Theology, Phoenix Seminary; Chaplain (Major), Air National Guard

The jury is in, and the verdict is clear. Most marriage partners are essentially incompatible according to the law. Thank God for grace . . . and for *The Grace Marriage*! As a professor and professional marriage and family therapist for over thirty years, I absolutely love this approach that weds grace and intentionality with smart training.

SCOTT WIGGINTON, LMFT, Professor of Pastoral Ministries & Counseling, Campbellsville University; Executive Director, Winterpast Counseling

This book gives us a clear reminder that the same grace that transforms our spiritual lives can also transform our marriages. God uses marriage to grow and mature us in ways that no other human relationship can. Brad and Marilyn's life and marriage are a testimony to the power of grace in action.

DEREK IRVIN, Marriage & Care Pastor, Northview Church

Brad and Marilyn don't just talk the talk, but they walk the walk. This book is not theoretical, it's full of practical and applicable coaching for all of us who want to glorify God in our marriages. I've seen them live it out in their own lives and highly recommend this book! Read it with your spouse!

KENT EVANS, Executive Director, Manhood Journey; author of *Bring Your Hammer: 28 Tools Dads Can Grab from the Book of Nehemiah*

THE

grace

marriage

How the Gospel
and Intentionality
Transform Your Relationship

FOREWORD BY DR. JULI SLATTERY

Brad and Marilyn Rhoads
with Brittany Cragg

MOODY PUBLISHERS
CHICAGO

© 2023 by
GRACE MARRIAGE

All rights reserved. No part of this book may be reproduced in any form without permission in writing from the publisher, except in the case of brief quotations embodied in critical articles or reviews.

Scripture quotations, unless otherwise noted, are from the ESV® Bible (The Holy Bible, English Standard Version®), copyright © 2001 by Crossway, a publishing ministry of Good News Publishers. Used by permission. All rights reserved. The ESV text may not be quoted in any publication made available to the public by a Creative Commons license. The ESV may not be translated into any other language.

Scripture quotations marked (NIV) are taken from the Holy Bible, New International Version®, NIV®. Copyright © 1973, 1978, 1984, 2011 by Biblica, Inc.™ Used by permission of Zondervan. All rights reserved worldwide. www.zondervan.com The "NIV" and "New International Version" are trademarks registered in the United States Patent and Trademark Office by Biblica, Inc.™

Scripture quotations marked (NLT) are taken from the *Holy Bible*, New Living Translation, copyright ©1996, 2004, 2015 by Tyndale House Foundation. Used by permission of Tyndale House Publishers, Carol Stream, Illinois 60188. All rights reserved.

Scripture quotations marked (AMPC) are taken from the Amplified ® Bible, Copyright © 1954, 1958, 1962, 1964, 1965, 1987 by The Lockman Foundation. Used by permission. www.lockman.org.

Some of the content in this book has previously been used in videos and workbooks from the ministry Grace Marriage (www.gracemarriage.com).

Emphasis to Scripture has been added.

Edited by Tim Grissom and Pam Pugh
Interior design: Puckett Smartt
Cover design: Clear Design Group
Brad and Marilyn Rhoads photo: Jamie Alexander / tannerwest.com
Brittany Cragg photo: Mallory Kee Photography

Library of Congress Cataloging-in-Publication Data

Names: Rhoads, Brad, 1968- author.
Title: The grace marriage : how the gospel and intentionality transform
  your relationship / Brad and Marilyn Rhoads with Brittany Tarr Cragg.
Description: Chicago : Moody Publishers, [2023] | Includes bibliographical
  references. | Summary: "How the Gospel and Intentionality Transform Your
  Relationship"-- Provided by publisher.
Identifiers: LCCN 2022038587 (print) | LCCN 2022038588 (ebook) | ISBN
  9780802421487 | ISBN 9780802473073 (ebook)
Subjects: LCSH: Marriage--Religious aspects--Christianity.
Classification: LCC BV4596.M3 R49 2023 (print) | LCC BV4596.M3 (ebook) |
  DDC 248.8/44--dc23/eng/20230126
LC record available at https://lccn.loc.gov/2022038587
LC ebook record available at https://lccn.loc.gov/2022038588

Originally delivered by fleets of horse-drawn wagons, the affordable paperbacks from D. L. Moody's publishing house resourced the church and served everyday people. Now, after more than 125 years of publishing and ministry, Moody Publishers' mission remains the same—even if our delivery systems have changed a bit. For more information on other books (and resources) created from a biblical perspective, go to www.moodypublishers.com or write to:

Moody Publishers
820 N. LaSalle Boulevard
Chicago, IL 60610

3 5 7 9 10 8 6 4 2

Printed in the United States of America

We dedicate this book to the legacy of the life of Doug Hignell. God gave Doug to the Rhoads family as a transformative force—a force full of grace, love, and generosity. Our prayer is that this book honors the legacy of this precious mentor, friend, and follower of Christ. We miss you, Doug, and thank God for our "family" in California.

Contents

Foreword

You have likely heard that nurturing your relationship with Jesus will strengthen your marriage. Maybe that sounds like super-spiritual and even hollow advice. What you really need is someone to teach your husband how to clean up after himself. The book you really want is the one that convicts your wife about her critical attitude. Seriously, how could knowing Jesus better help with the everyday problems of sexual incompatibility, an empty bank account, difficult children, and conflict over housework?

This book proposes the radical idea that knowing Christ Jesus as your Savior and Lord can and must totally transform your marriage.

In my experience, most Christians approach marriage with the same mindset as the larger culture. Yes, we may sprinkle some "holy water" on our marriages by praying now and then, attending church together, and putting a plaque of 1 Corinthians 13 on the bathroom wall. But in every practical way, in every way that matters, Jesus Christ is an *observer* rather than a *transformer* of our marriages.

Yet God calls His children to live profoundly transformed lives in every arena—including (and especially!) marriage. The Christian marriage is not a sanctified contract ensuring happiness. Instead, it is a call to lifelong covenant with another person.

It's difficult to overestimate how much contract or performance thinking has impacted our marriages. I've seen this to be true in my own union of twenty-eight years. When my husband doesn't love me as I believe he should, it's natural for me to withdraw or even punish him to get his attention. That formula might be common sense, but it isn't God's way. Jesus said as much: even a pagan can love those who love them (see Matt. 5:46–47)!

God's call for a Christian husband and wife goes far beyond how the world defines marital love. His design is that we extend the same love, the same grace, the same forgiveness, and the same faithfulness that God Himself has given us.

If that seems overwhelming or impossible to you, you are not alone. But what is impossible with man is possible with God. This book does more than tell you how to *do* marriage right. Instead, it is a roadmap on how to *become* the husband or wife God calls you to be.

Don't be fooled into thinking that the road to a holy marriage is one of drudgery and duty. As you will see through Brad and Marilyn's candid testimony, God's design for a grace-filled marriage has the potential to be the most joyful relationship imaginable.

And as for my experience with Brad and Marilyn, let me tell you—every word you read and every story they tell is the real deal. They faithfully live out the message of grace they teach.

The Rhoads are passionate about Jesus; He transformed their marriage and wants to do the same for you. It is a joy for me to count them as friends and partners in ministry, and I am confident the gospel hope they share here for marriages will bless you, too.

DR. JULI SLATTERY
President and cofounder of Authentic Intimacy
Author of *God, Sex, and Your Marriage*

1

Great Love Stories Can Have Ugly Beginnings

On our twentieth anniversary, I told Marilyn, "This has been the best twenty years of my life."

She responded, "It's been the best nineteen of mine. There's no way I'm giving you that first year!"

Decades of marriage and five children later, I'm thankful for God's kindness to us in saving our marriage after a nearly disastrous beginning.

Our story begins in Nashville, Tennessee, in 1995.

I had just gotten back to the office where I was working as an attorney. I'd derailed my schedule by locking my keys in my car after meeting with a client in Waco (the one in Tennessee, not the one in Texas). Disheveled and harried, I finally dragged myself through the office door around 10:00 that night.

Then I saw her.

She was sitting in a paralegal's office, working on her résumé.

Her long brown hair fell down around her shoulders, shining against the backdrop of a blue business suit. She was stunning.

She turned and looked at me as I walked by, and my feet almost involuntarily turned into that office. I chatted with her and the paralegal, who was her sister, for nearly an hour. I later learned that her sister told her, "I've worked here for three years, and that guy hasn't talked to me for five minutes the entire time."

I was smitten.

A few months later, I saw her in the office again, and this time, I was a little bolder. I said, "Hey, if you ever want to go for a run or something, give me a call."

She paused, handed me her business card, and said, "If you ever want to go on a run, you give *me* a call."

She later told her roommate, "I've met a really interesting guy, but he asked *me* to call *him* if I wanted to hang out . . . so he's either cocky or he has a girlfriend." And she was right. I was dating someone else at the time and was trying to assuage a guilty conscience.

After the other relationship ended, I decided I was not going to date for a year. But then I remembered Marilyn. *One date couldn't hurt, right?* I called and asked if she'd still like to go on that run. We agreed to make it a hike instead so we could talk.

Given all I did wrong on our first date, it's nothing short of a miracle that she ended up marrying me. After work that evening, she drove to my house to change clothes. When she went into the bathroom to change, it was so gross she dry-heaved . . . twice.

I told her we'd take my truck. Since I was an attorney at a big firm, she expected a nice SUV. Instead, she slid into my dirty, turquoise, extended cab Ford Ranger. The interior was filthy; my black lab's hair was everywhere. She even found a dog hair in the ice cube in her cup. I didn't open the door for her, and had to scramble to throw out a beer can and cup of tobacco spit before she got in. On the drive home, my dog sat in the space behind the seat and hung his head over Marilyn's lap, showering her legs with slobber.

When we got back to my house, we decided to go out to dinner. Marilyn wanted to go home and change her clothes first, but I was hungry. So even though I took the time to change into something nicer, she had to go in the same shorts and T-shirt she'd worn on the hike.

> *Obviously, God had ordained that we should be together. There is no other rational explanation for why she didn't run the other way.*

After dinner, we hung out for a while with my roommate. She sat on one end of the couch, and I sat on the other. I was intrigued by how she looked right at me when I talked. My roommate even commented on it later. Guys like us weren't used to good eye-to-eye communication.

I think you're getting the picture. She was out of my league, in looks and in pretty much all levels of maturity. I was onto something really good, and I knew it.

Marilyn was everything I wanted. She was strong in her faith and bold in her moral convictions. Unlike me, she had a past to be proud of. Right away, I knew I would have to make changes if this relationship was going to have a chance. I stopped my bad habits immediately. I thought, *I am not going to lose the best thing that has ever happened to me for things that aren't good for me.*

For her part, Marilyn went home from our first date and

(shockingly) told her roommate that it was the best first date she had ever had! Dog slobber and all. She was actually impressed that I didn't try to be impressive.

Obviously, God had ordained that we should be together. There is no other rational explanation for why she didn't run the other way.

Thus began our whirlwind courtship.

. . . .

I (Marilyn) have to speak up here. We've had our marital difficulties—and we'll get to that later—but Brad was amazing at dating. He made me feel like the most special person in the world. He opened doors for me (after the first date, at least), bought me flowers, and paid a lot of money for small portions of pretty food because he knew it'd make me feel valued. We talked on the phone or in person every day. I never had to pry to get him talking on a heart-to-heart level. He was an open book.

We wrote love notes and hid them for the other to find, tried to outdo each other in planning fun dates, and surprised each other with gifts. I once left a note under his windshield wipers that said, "*You stumped me, Brad Rhoads.*" He wasn't totally sure what I meant, but I didn't know how to explain it. He was unlike anyone I'd ever met. We were absolutely crazy about each other.

At one point, we went out twenty-four nights in a row. Our relationship was booming while bank accounts and work production were going the opposite direction.

Three months after our first date, Brad asked me to marry him. It was a joy to accept.

. . . .

I (Brad) remember checking my bank account before buying an engagement ring and realizing I was going to spend nearly all my money on her ring. No more emergency funds. No more savings. *Who cares? I get to marry Marilyn!* Nothing else in life seemed to matter.

During our engagement, we thought it would be a good idea to go to a marriage conference. We bought tickets with high hopes, but the first day, the speakers talked about how to navigate differences and struggles in marriage. It took us all of thirty minutes to realize the speakers didn't understand our relationship, so we left and did not return. Why spend two days listening to stuff that didn't apply to us? *We'd do anything for each other. We would never hurt each other!* But we agreed it was good they had stuff like that for people who needed it.

After a quick, four-month engagement, we were married. And we have had a fun and blissfully easy marriage ever since.

Just. Kidding.

We didn't learn how wrong we were about marriage until we got married.

THE REALITY OF MARRIAGE

Due to our speedy courtship, neither one of us had the opportunity to really get to know the other, nor to observe how we behaved in real life. The rose-colored glasses fell off quickly. Marilyn first glimpsed grouchy Brad at our wedding reception when I wheeled around and snapped with sarcasm at the photographer (who was a dear friend of Marilyn's family) as we got in the car for our send-off: "Why don't we just stop here so you can take one more picture?"

As for our honeymoon, Marilyn tells people that the honeymoon was over before the honeymoon was over. We learned quickly that marriage is really nothing like dating; it's a whole new deal. Living together, sexual freedom, merged finances, annoying habits, and all our sins and struggles became an instant reality. For some, the first year is easy. For us, within six months, I went from Marilyn's favorite person to her least favorite person. Her perception of me went from "no one has ever loved me like this" to "no one has ever hurt me like this."

As Marilyn describes it now, I was great at dating, but pretty horrible at being married. For one thing, my creative energy for her immediately shut down, as I turned my attention away from her and toward building a law practice. Right away, I signed us up for a 35-week bowling league so I could meet people and get new clients. Marilyn hated everything about it. She hated bowling, our dorky, turquoise team shirts, and the building itself, which reeked of smoke. It didn't help that the team was really competitive and that she was not very good at bowling. When she'd throw a bad ball, no one on the team would even make eye contact with her. (One of our teammates asked her to work on her hand strength and gave her bowling videos to watch.) Immune to her distress, I continued to focus on expanding my clientele.

Not only did I ask her to spend her free time doing things she hated for my benefit, I filled any extra downtime with everything *but* her. I was obsessed with sports. On multiple occasions, I went to watch high school football games—where I didn't know anyone on either team—leaving her at home alone on a Friday night. Sunny Saturdays found me inside all day, watching sports on TV and simultaneously listening to sports talk radio, while Marilyn mowed the lawn, tended the garden, or cleaned the house.

I was irresponsible on many levels. I was, to put it gently, a slob. I remember Marilyn telling me, "It's one thing to leave the soap in the bottom of the tub, but the wrapper too?" She was gone for a week on a work trip once; when she returned, she knew every outfit I'd worn that week from the five different piles on our bedroom floor.

I didn't steward her heart, or my own, very well. When she'd get upset, I'd tell her to go to the bathroom and look for the chill pills. Or I might engage her least favorite hand signal of all time: hands up in surrender, then slowly bringing them down while mouthing, "*Calm down.*" When we were looking for a new church home, she would meet with the pastors alone. I just told her I was okay with whatever church she liked best.

In dating, I had treated Marilyn like the most special woman in the world. I pursued her at every level. She knew, beyond a shadow of a doubt, that she was my number one priority. Then, I took my foot off the pedal as soon as we got married.

Marilyn was struggling. She had made significant sacrifices for me. Just before our wedding, I had agreed to launch a branch office of my father and uncle's law practice. That's why, when our honeymoon was over, Marilyn and I came back to a new house in a brand-new town. Marilyn had to leave Nashville—a place she loved, a job she loved, and friends she loved—to move to Owensboro, Kentucky, a place where she knew no one, where there was little to do, and where, were it not for me, she would have zero desire to be.

She needed a caring, attentive husband to help her adjust. But she didn't have one.

She vividly remembers asking the Lord at one point, "Am I sentenced to a life of this?"

Marilyn felt neglected . . . because she *was* neglected. I was aloof and preoccupied with myself. She was clearly unhappy with me and our marriage, but I couldn't understand why. My staff liked me. My clients liked me. My law practice was growing. I was respected in our community. Hey, I even won the Volunteer of the Year award in our town. I thought, *What is her problem? Is everyone else wrong about me?*

I knew our relationship wasn't doing well, and I blamed her. I truly thought our primary problem was a hypersensitive wife. I thought, *If she'd quit making such a big deal about everything, we'd be fine!*

For most of that first year, we lived parallel lives. I was building a law practice; she was getting a graduate degree. I didn't realize how lonely she was, but I'd get glimpses of her deep sadness. When she would sometimes just start crying, I'd get frustrated with her: "Why are you crying? I didn't do anything!"

That was the point . . . I wasn't doing anything.

A CHANGE OF HEARTS

Our marriage began to transform one night when Marilyn came to me and said, "We need to talk."

Then it got worse: "Brad, I don't need you." That felt like a kick to the chest. My whole life hung on her next words . . . "I want to ask for your forgiveness. I have been asking from you what only God can give me. My joy and identity don't depend on you. My fulfillment in everything only comes from Jesus. I will love you the way He is calling me to love you, but

I am off your roller coaster."

Through spending time with the Lord over the course of a few weeks, she had come to a new understanding of the amazing sufficiency of Christ. God had been reassuring her that He was enough. She didn't need me for happiness in any area of her life. She had everything she needed in Him.

It was freeing for Marilyn to realize that her joy didn't hinge on how good of a husband I was, that it depended instead on the perfect, consistent, lavish love of Jesus. She learned she could be incredibly happy and content even if her husband was self-absorbed and clueless (my words, not hers).

In the following weeks, our marriage shifted from rocky to stable. I admired the new peace about Marilyn, a persistent light that brightened everything she did. Ours still wasn't a great marriage, though, because it still had one huge problem in it . . . me.

Selfishness still blinded me. In fact, I was too blind to even know I had blind spots. I didn't see a need to change.

My uncle saw it, though. He could tell I was succeeding in everything except what mattered most. He invited me numerous times to a men's conference focused on marriage. Each time, I made an excuse. Finally, he called Marilyn and cleared the weekend on our calendar. Then, he called my office manager and cleared my schedule. He followed up by buying my ticket *and* inviting my father-in-law to come too. After all that, he called me. Every time I tried to make an excuse, he'd say, "I already checked. You are clear."

By nature, I run high on energy and short on attention. Sitting through a one-hour church service can be rough. Eight hours of marriage "preaching" in a room with thousands of other dudes sounded horrific. Besides, I didn't need marriage advice; I needed someone to tell my wife to relax.

Little did I know what God had in store for me.

I remember moments from that conference like it happened yesterday. Scripture is truly a double-edged sword, and I was cut to the bone. One of the speakers read Ephesians 5:25: "Husbands, love your wives, as Christ loved the church and gave himself up for her" and then asked, "How much do you give up for your wife?"

Little did I know what God had in store for me.

Ummm ... nothing.

"Live with your wives in an understanding way" (1 Peter 3:7) was followed by, "Do you get into her world, listen to her, and seek to really understand and love her?"

No, never.

"Husbands, love your wives, and do not be harsh with them" (Col. 3:19).

I am sarcastic and rude to her often.

The realization struck me that I probably treated her worse than I treated anyone else.

On the long ride home, I reflected on how I'd left for the conference thinking I was a pretty great husband and was returning thinking that I wasn't doing anything well at all. I felt, with bittersweet gratitude, that God had given me discipline I hadn't known I needed. Although it crushed me to realize how I had treated an amazing daughter of God so terribly, I couldn't wait to get home and start loving her well. I was so thankful Marilyn was still my wife. I had time to make this right!

It was well into early morning hours when I got home. I

woke Marilyn and told her, "The conference was amazing, and I am so sorry for the way I've treated you. The only thing that is going to be different from here on out is *everything*."

I was learning the truth of 2 Corinthians 7:10–11:

> Godly sorrow brings repentance that leads to salvation and leaves no regret, but worldly sorrow brings death. See what this godly sorrow has produced in you: what earnestness, what eagerness to clear yourselves, what indignation, what alarm, what longing, what concern, what readiness to see justice done. (NIV)

I was eager to right all I had done wrong; I was ready to begin loving my wife as Scripture commanded me to. God wasn't punishing me or beating me down; He had graciously revealed His truth to me so I could draw closer to Him and my wife.

The next morning at about 5:30, Marilyn got up to plant flowers before church. Although I had only been in bed a few hours, I thought, *it's time to get started.* I walked outside, grabbed a shovel, looked her in the face, and asked, "Where do you want me to dig?"

She very nearly passed out. I had never gotten up early with her. I certainly had never offered to help her garden. I reminded her of my words in the middle of the night—things were going to be different.

"I'm starting right now," I told her. "So, where do you want me to dig?"

MARRIAGES NEED HELP AND HOPE

Since that morning in our front yard, things really have been different. Our marriage has not been perfect, whatever that means, but it has been pretty amazing.

Even with having five kids and multiple life crises, we have, almost without exception, gone on a weekly date for over twenty-five years. We keep short accounts (meaning we try to resolve conflict quickly), extend grace, and have a blast together. Now we get to spend our lives helping other couples experience this kind of transformation.

How do we make our marriages better than "we're all right; everything's fine"?

A quick look around shows that marriage transformation is sorely needed. Cohabitation is commonplace, divorce is prevalent, pornography is squelching the life and health from men, women, and their marriages. Monogamy is even considered taboo in some circles.

The church is no exception. For many, marriage is something to whine about, not rejoice over. Even marriages that seem generally okay are also kind of stale. An affectionate, fun, life-giving marriage has been relegated to some cute anomaly.

Many churches have no dedicated marriage ministry. Those that do tend to relegate marriage ministry to either premarital or crisis counseling. There is a sore lack of outreach to marriages that are neither thriving nor in flames.

We all know this is not how God intended it to be. If God designed marriage, then He designed it to be very, very good.

How do we get there? What are we to do when we feel stuck in a rut of complacency? How do we make our marriages better than "we're all right; everything's fine"? How can we show the world the beauty of God's design for marriage—and have a lot of fun while doing so?

Grab a shovel. Let's start digging.

DIGGING IN TO GRACE + INTENTIONALITY

We've found that there's often a disconnect between teaching and implementation. Great sermons, books, and conferences rarely translate into real, lasting change in how couples approach life and marriage. So, at the end of each chapter, we'll provide some questions for your consideration and reflection as a pathway to implementation and growth.

We pray this space at the end of each chapter doesn't feel like a quiz or a box to check off, but rather helps your marriage grow in grace and enjoyment.

What characteristics first attracted you to your spouse?

1.
2.
3.
4.
5.

What do you remember about first meeting your spouse, or about your first date?

1.

2.

3.

4.

5.

What are some of the fun things you used to do while dating, or in the early years of your marriage, that you've stopped doing?

1.

2.

3.

4.

5.

The Performance-Based Marriage:
Where Your Best Is Never Enough

When Marilyn and I first got married, I didn't think, *Now that I'm married, I'll be rude, slop up the house, join a bowling league so I don't spend time with her, go to games all the time, and see how miserable I can make her.* I had wrong thinking about myself and marriage, and that led to wrong behavior. I needed an entirely different perspective.

When we're seeking to grow in some area, it can be helpful to first discover where our thinking got off track. We can then discard wrong thinking and behavior and start anew. If the well of joy is running dry in your marriage, let's get rid of the stagnant stuff before you attempt to put fresh water in.

If your marriage alternates between feeling okay and feeling burdensome, you may be living in a performance-based marriage. And if that's true, your marriage is like most marriages out there.

WHAT IS A PERFORMANCE-BASED MARRIAGE?

In a performance-based marriage, love is given and withdrawn by one spouse based on the behavior of the other. For example, if your spouse is nice and takes good care of you, then you will be nice and care for them. If your spouse is unkind or thought-less, you'll snap back or go cold. You will respond to their failure with withdrawal or consequences.

The fuel for a performance-based marriage is effort. If both spouses perform well, then the marriage performs well. But problematically, fuel levels run low at times. When the perfor-mance of either spouse dips, the marriage suffers.

When Marilyn and I are in performance mode, here's what our marriage can look like.

Let's say Marilyn gets overwhelmed with some (or all) of our five kids. When she is struggling, she'll raise her voice at the kids and tell me how I am either not helping or am making the problem worse. Her volume level tends to increase with her stress level.

If I'm in performance mode, I get defensive and tell her to calm down. Then I, too, get short with the kids. I go quiet and withdraw, making sure she gets the message that I am annoyed.

You can guess how well this works in helping Marilyn to a better place.

Since I've added insult to injury, Marilyn is now hurt *and* angry, and she withdraws from me. She doesn't want to be around me, and the feeling is mutual. A cold distance sets in.

In a performance-based marriage, love must be earned. It is a reward, not a gift.

LIFE IN PERFORMANCE MODE

Performance-based marriages are prevalent because we live in a performance-based world. Rewards and consequences are doled out based on how well we do. While this may be necessary in the marketplace, it is not the way gospel love works. In marriage, we almost subconsciously give and take away love based on how we feel we are being treated. We withhold love because we don't want bad behavior to continue, or we give it as a reward because we are pleased and desire more of that good behavior.

Of course, there can be a beautiful synergy in marriage where love motivates love, and sacrifice motivates sacrifice. However, when one spouse struggles and the other pulls back, bitterness takes root in the gap.

In performance mode, we reserve our precious resources of heart and soul for those we deem truly deserving.

You don't get my affection today; that is reserved for Good Wife.

You don't get my respect today; only Nice Husband gets that.

Of course, we would never say such things out loud. But this manner of thinking sometimes undergirds our behavior toward our spouse. This is the familiar notion of quid pro quo. You scratch my back, I'll scratch yours. You give me what I want, I'll give you what you want.

You can hear the idolatry of self in that line of thinking. Galatians 5:17 tells us, "For the desires of the flesh are against the Spirit, and the desires of the Spirit are against the flesh, for these are opposed to each other, to keep you from doing the things you want to do." The pull of our flesh is powerful, and the thing the flesh loves most is itself. Operating in the flesh will push you toward a performance-based marriage, where your focus is always on what your spouse should be doing better.

This default selfishness keeps our finger pointed at anyone but ourselves for the cause of our relational issues. We may think, *If my husband would just be more helpful around the house, I would have more energy for him, and we would have a better marriage.* Or, *If my wife wasn't so stingy sexually, I wouldn't be frustrated with her all the time, and we would have a better marriage.*

Even our relationship with God can suffer from a performance-based mentality. Consider how we frequently equate how much God loves us with how we are behaving. Our peace levels can be determined more by how *we* think we are doing than by *His* grace. We can focus more on what we have done than on what Christ accomplished on the cross. It's as though our joy and contentment hinge on whether we are on God's "good boy" or "good girl" list.

We know that's not right, but we still often feel that way.

• • • •

Before we go further, please understand this: Avoiding a performance-based marriage *does not* include tolerating abuse of any kind or infidelity (we'll talk more about this in chapter 3). In these situations, safety must be prioritized, and counsel must be sought.

Also, nothing in this chapter should imply that you shouldn't communicate with your spouse about things you do and don't appreciate. Grace is not ignoring issues and pretending everything is okay. We'll address communication lines later, but open communication and regular connection are a must.

THE HAMSTER WHEEL OF PERFORMANCE

The obvious problem with a performance-based marriage is that, as in our relationship with God, a standard of perfect performance is unattainable.

When Brad and I condition our love on the performance of the other, we are placing our marriage under the law. We are implying that the other must meet the requirements of Brad's Law or Marilyn's Law in order to be in good standing. And when we begin to put laws into our marriage that we expect the other to uphold, we set each other up to fail.

> Over time, spouses in a performance-based marriage learn to live separate lives. Instead of growing in enjoying each other, they grow in tolerating each other.

Second Corinthians 3:6 says that "the letter [of the law] kills, but the Spirit gives life." Paul refers to the law as the ministry of death and condemnation,[1] because it will always show us how far we have fallen from the mark.[2] The verdict on our performance according to the law will always be *Guilty.* Failed. Did Not Finish.

When we set up laws in marriage, we bring distance and condemnation into the relationship. We hold sin and mistakes against each other. Resentment grows. Soon, sin has dominion over the marriage, as both spouses insist on choosing themselves over the other.

You may have a period where you both intentionally try hard, and your marriage is better for a while. Then, a mistake or

---

1. See 2 Corinthians 3:7, 9.
2. Romans 5:20.

argument blows everything to pieces. Sunken frustrations and despair are dredged to the surface. You feel discouraged and ashamed over having landed back where you began. You hop back on the hamster wheel and resolve to do better next time.

Over time, spouses in a performance-based marriage learn to live separate lives. Instead of growing in *enjoying* each other, they grow in *tolerating* each other. She gets to a point where she feels she can live with his issues, and everything is okay. He does the same. They choose a shallow coexistence over meaningful intimacy for the sake of the peace—which really isn't peace at all. But the hamster wheel still sits in the shadows, waiting for one of them to mess up again. One bad fight can send them spinning for weeks.

As we focus on our own performance and the performance of our spouse, our marriage will rise and fall with our circumstances. Our marriage will be self-centered and self-dependent, instead of God-centered and God-dependent. Marriage will be a duty, not a delight.

In the same way, our relationship with God will be doomed if we seek to build it on our own efforts instead of the perfection of Jesus. When we seek to work our way into God's favor, we place ourselves under the law. We come up with grand plans to do right and avoid wrong, like getting a new Bible reading plan, journal, or accountability partner.

Yet we still find ourselves cycling through the same old sin patterns. And we feel the same grudging disappointment from God. It's the same hamster wheel as in our human relationships, but the stakes are much higher.

The law will tell you—every time—that you are not enough. Not enough for your spouse, not enough for God.

FREED FROM THE WHACK-A-MOLE GAME

I (Brad) have learned the hard way that trying to be enough in your own strength can nearly kill you. For years, I focused more on trying to be a good Christian than I did on Christ Himself. I tried, through various means of self-improvement, to make myself more pleasing to God. I got more involved in our church. I studied the Bible. I taught. I preached. Marilyn and I counseled other couples. Eventually, I was ordained as an elder. But I wasn't really growing in the fruit of the Spirit. I was reading more, but I wasn't more patient. I was giving more, but I wasn't gentler. I was helping more people, but I wasn't more joyful.

Honestly, following Jesus felt heavy, hard, and full of pressure. I was painfully aware of several areas where I fell short, and life felt like an endless game of whack-a-mole: Identify sin or area of needed growth. Establish a plan to do better. Execute. And no sooner did I feel I'd made progress in one area than another Bradism would pop up, and I'd set to work on that one.

I believed the Bible. All of it. But passages about an easy yoke, light burden, rest for our souls,[3] a Sabbath rest for the people of God,[4] being anxious about nothing[5] . . . those verses didn't sound like my life at all.

In my faith and in my family life, my peace and happiness depended on my performance. If I read my Bible and prayed, was productive at work, was nice to Marilyn, exercised, and ate reasonably well, then I felt good about myself. I slept soundly. If I missed my quiet time, had conflict with Marilyn, or

3. Matthew 11:29–30.
4. Hebrews 4:9–10.
5. Philippians 4:6.

got distracted at work, I'd go to bed feeling miserable—not just about what I thought I had done wrong, but about *everything*.

My only solution for the tension I felt was to try harder. In every area of life, I was driven to be better and do more. More reading. More prayer. More work. More spiritual impact. More teaching. More service. More giving. More time with Marilyn. More time with each of the kids.

Does any of this sound familiar to you?

While each of those things was good to pursue, focusing on them consumed me.

One night as I lay in bed, with my heart and my mind trying to outrace each other, I could hardly breathe. I woke Marilyn and told her I might be having a heart attack. After a midnight trip to the ER and a heart catheterization, I was released on the doctor's strong suggestion that I reduce stress in my life. My quest to white-knuckle my way into being a better Christian and a better spouse needed to end.

Shortly afterward, in a quiet moment with God, I heard Him *almost audibly* say: "Brad, you are not okay . . . and that's okay. I love you. You are My son." In that moment, I felt freed from the constant pressure to do more and be more that had marked my life. I felt His grace over me. It was as if a bag of bricks had been lifted from my back. For the first time in a long time, I could breathe deeply.

THE GREAT HOPE FOR BAD PERFORMERS

That encounter with God convinced me that I had been drawing my hope and strength from the wrong source.

Our hope in daily life is not in behaving so well that we

land a spot on God's "good" list. Our hope in marriage is not in striving to become the ideal mate. Our hope in *every sphere* is the great hope we hold for eternity—Christ has paid it all, for each of us.

God walked the earth as a perfect man and took our sins upon Himself at the cross. He defeated the power of sin and death for all time when He rose again three days later. Those who, by faith, call Him Lord of their lives and trust His grace *alone* for their salvation are given the free gifts of full forgiveness and eternal life.

In other words, it's not up to us to become acceptable to Him or to be approved by Him. He has already taken care of all of that.

It is finished.

Ephesians 2:8–9 could not be more clear: "For by grace you have been saved through faith. *And this is not your own doing; it is the gift of God, not a result of works, so that no one may boast.*" We don't curry favor with God and earn His approval. Our good days do not make Him love us more. Our worst days do not make Him love us less. Nothing we do has any effect on His steadfast affection for us.

> **Our good days do not make God love us more. Our worst days do not make Him love us less.**

Colossians 2:13–14 tells us why: "And you, who were dead in your trespasses and the uncircumcision of your flesh, God made alive together with [Jesus], having forgiven us all our trespasses, by canceling the record of debt that stood against us with its legal demands. This he set aside, nailing it to the cross."

This is the good news of the gospel. We don't have to get cleaned up before we come to God. He chose us and canceled the record of our sin when we had nothing to offer because we were *dead*. God's heart toward us is like that of the father in the parable of the prodigal son.[6]

Though his son had been offensive and foolish (and likely reeked of pig feces), the father *ran* to him when he saw him coming. The father embraced him, threw a party for him, and restored him to full sonship. Nothing the son had done could deter the gracious, celebratory, unstoppable love of the father.

For those who have put their faith in Christ's redeeming work, God sees the all-sufficient blood of Jesus when He looks at you. He is perfectly just, and He will always honor the atonement His blameless Son made on your behalf. If you are Christ's, you have been made a new man or woman *in Christ*.

You are no longer under the law. You are under grace.

THIS GRACE IS REALLY GOOD NEWS

God's grace is hard to fathom, but if we seek to grasp it, it is good news that can change the rest of our lives. A grace-filled focus will keep us close to the heart of God as we joyfully lean on Him, rather than ourselves, to supply our needs.

And grace can *completely* revolutionize your marriage.

Release yourself from the burden of striving for perfection in your own power. Rest in God's grace toward you. Trust the unfathomable freedom available in the forgiveness of Jesus. Then, with a rested and grateful soul, you can enjoy the nourishing fruits of the Spirit and exhibit them to your spouse.

Two believers who are resting in the grace of Christ and

---

6. See Luke 15:11–32.

extending that same grace to each other tend to get along pretty well.

You will continue to sin against, hurt, and frustrate each other, but sin doesn't have to dictate your marriage nor the atmosphere of your home. Romans 6:14 says, "For sin will have no dominion over you [and your marriage], since you [and your marriage] are not under *law* but under *grace.*"

Notice what the Bible does *not* say. It does not say, "Sin will have no dominion over you because you will become so strong and holy that you will never stumble or struggle again." No! Sin will be a reality this side of heaven. But because you are under God's grace, sin has no power to enslave you. Sin cannot lay claim to that which it does not own.

This is also true for our marriages. Sin will have no control over a marriage under grace. And what does a marriage under grace look like, practically speaking?

We're so glad you asked.

DIGGING IN TO GRACE + INTENTIONALITY

What does your spouse tend to do (or not do) that can prompt you to retaliate or withdraw?

1.
2.
3.
4.
5.

What behaviors can you change or omit that tend to push you and your spouse into the performance trap?

1.

2.

3.

4.

5.

Are there areas of your life where you need to confess wrong thinking about God's grace to Him, or even to your spouse?

3

The Grace-Based Marriage:
Where Love Covers a Multitude of Sins

If we are in the habit of giving love and affection based on behavior, how do we step into an entirely different paradigm? In other words, how do we jump off the hamster wheel of performance—and stay off?

Answer: by receiving and extending the incredible grace of God.

WHAT GRACE IS

In a grace-based marriage, the spouses get grace. I mean, they *really* get it.

When you understand the grace you were shown at the cross, when you accept and receive forgiveness and favor, then you are able to give with abandon that which you have received. Grace begets grace.

You did not and cannot earn God's love and grace, it is a gift. It is free. Jesus commands us to love each other like He loves us,[1] so spouses under grace do not love each other based on merit or performance. Each spouse loves the other freely, regardless of their behavior.

Grace responds to bad with good, as Jesus did. "But God shows his love for us in that *while we were still sinners*, Christ died for us."[2] God didn't evaluate us and then think, "Wow, that one is impressive! I think I'll save that one." He saw selfishness and rebellion in each one, then sacrificed His Son to save and set us free.

We are told to love each other like that.

So, when your spouse sins against you, *before* they come clean and apologize, put self aside and show them love.

The grace-based marriage doesn't thrive because each spouse works hard to achieve "star spouse" status. It isn't tethered at all to the unsynchronized roller coasters of his-and-her behavior. A grace-based marriage thrives because of the perfection of Jesus, not the efforts of the spouses. It is built securely on the rock of Christ.

In my own strength, I easily get overwhelmed with all there is to be done and I become anxious and irritable. Sometimes I'll try to keep it all in, but eventually my bubble bursts and all the unpleasantness spills out.

Recently, I got into an intense exchange with one of our adult daughters. I handled it poorly. She handled it poorly. We

---

1. John 13:34; 15:12.
2. Romans 5:8.

both would have been embarrassed if you had witnessed it. Marilyn's struggles look different. She gets sad, tearful, and really stressed. Like getting-shingles-twice-in-one-year kind of stress. It is obvious she is struggling when her volume goes up and she starts saying the same thing over and over with increasing intensity.

The reality is: We wish we handled life well all the time, but we just don't. Yet, for the most part, we have great family relationships.

Why? Because we understand grace. We don't hold sin against each other. We are reminded how God forgives us. Then, we offer that forgiveness to each other. We choose to move on and enjoy each other. The truth of Romans 6:14 plays out beautifully; sin has no mastery, control, or dominion. We are not under the law, but under grace.

Now, about the exchange between me and my daughter. Within an hour, we were hanging out and laughing together. I repented and accepted the grace of God. She repented and accepted the grace of God. I gave her grace. She gave me grace. Then, guess what? The ministry of reconciliation had done its work. Sin had no control. We were close again.

Perhaps that sounds too good to be true, but when our human acts of grace are fueled by the power of the gospel, the gospel provides much greater power than most of us realize.

HOW GRACE WORKS

Practically, a grace-based marriage involves responding to sin or struggle with kindness and pursuit instead of consequences and distance. Grace moves us to offer service, kindness, time, and yes, even sex as free gifts to display the love of Jesus to our spouse.

If your spouse goes cold and gives you the silent treatment, respond by serving and blessing them.

If your spouse says something hurtful or makes a mistake, don't withhold your heart or your body.

If your spouse nags at you, be responsive and kind instead of snappy or sullen.

This sort of marriage puts the proverb into practice: "Whoever covers an offense seeks love."[3] And, when we adopt this approach, we often see the truth of Romans 2:4 lived out: "God's kindness is meant to lead you to repentance."

But we'll tell you from experience, grace can be tough to give *and* tough to receive, especially when you're new at this approach.

If Brad was harsh or did something to annoy me, my first thought wasn't, *My poor Brad is having a hard time. I just really want to bless him right now. We should go have sex.* Grace doesn't always sound like the right answer when you're in a bad mood.

When Brad was stressed and irritable, he didn't naturally want to say, "Marilyn, I know I am really cranky right now; thank you for being so kind and helpful in the midst of my struggle."

At first, grace is tough because we are hardwired to want to give people what they deserve. But be encouraged; the more

---

3. Proverbs 17:9.

you pursue grace and extend it, the easier and easier it becomes. No longer are you dominated by your own frustrations. When you shift into a grace approach, your focus is off your own offense, and on to how you can help each other.

It gets to be pretty fun.

I enjoy loving Brad. When he is struggling, I am challenged to creatively help instead of fruitlessly complain. This is much more effec-

> *The more you pursue grace and extend it, the easier and easier it becomes.*

tive (for both of us) than getting caught up in my head with the old "well, this stinks for me" approach.

Look at the following illustrations. Note how a performance-based marriage is doomed for distance or death, but a grace-based marriage keeps the couple close to each other and close to the heart of God.

Let's say I get frustrated over Brad's messiness and say, "I feel like I am raising six kids instead of five. You don't help at all around the house!" Then I live with low-grade anger toward him for a while. When I do this, I move away from him.

Performance-Based Marriage

FRUSTRATED
FEELS LIKE SHE HAS NO HELP
ANGER TOWARD HUSBAND

In a performance-based marriage, the husband (Brad in this example) would defend himself, feel unappreciated, withdraw from his wife, or give her a consequence, like snapping at her or lecturing her. When he does this, he moves away from his wife.

DEFENSIVE
FEELS UNAPPRECIATED
WITHDRAWS FROM WIFE

There is now a growing chasm between the husband and wife. They are frustrated with each other, and both hold sin against the other. Their hearts are separated by anger and resentment. Sin now has control over the marriage.

sin

In a grace-based marriage, the couple still sin against each other, but conflict and failure look different.

Again, let's say the wife takes offense at something the husband does and withdraws from him in anger again.

Grace-Based Marriage

FRUSTRATED
FEELS LIKE SHE HAS NO HELP
ANGER TOWARD HUSBAND

But here is where the progression shifts. Instead of taking offense or withdrawing, the husband extends grace and pursues his wife. He moves toward her. He loves her as he has been loved by God.

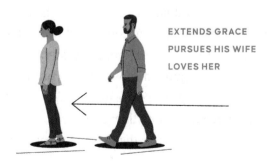

EXTENDS GRACE
PURSUES HIS WIFE
LOVES HER

The relational chasm that sin created is closed. Christ's ministry of reconciliation is put on display. The wife is helped out of her struggle. The gospel is lived out in marriage and, as often happens, kindness leads to repentance.

RECONCILED   GOSPEL LIVED OUT

Will You Love or Lecture?

The moment you feel offended is when you've arrived at the fork in the road. You'll know when it happens—often you can actually feel a point of decision inside.

At this moment, you can go one of two ways. You can strike back, go cold, and put your marriage on a rough path for a while. Or you can extend grace, be kind, pursue, and help.

First Corinthians 13:5 says love "is not touchy or fretful or resentful; it takes no account of the evil done to it [it pays no attention to a suffered wrong]" (AMPC).

Choosing grace means putting your offense aside and recognizing that your spouse needs *help* when they are struggling. They need love more than a lecture.

We like to call this the "rescue mentality."

Rescue Mentality > Offense Mentality

When your spouse is struggling, and it's manifesting in a short temper, gloominess, distance, or even just thoughtlessness, think of them as having fallen into a ditch and being unable to get out.

How would it sound for you to say: "How did you fall in that ditch again? Are you just dumb? And you look pathetic, the way you're trying to get out. If you ever do get out and clean yourself up, come talk to me."

You wouldn't say this. You would throw them a rope or do what you could to help them get out of that ditch.

Rescue—which is an act of grace—brings about change. But condemnation and contempt can kill a marriage.

Remember the words of Ecclesiastes: "Two are better than one. . . . If either of them falls down, one can help the other up. But pity anyone who falls and has no one to help them up."[4] A beautiful gift of marriage is that we have someone to help us up when we fall.

Love, sacrifice, grace, and pursuit (loving like Jesus does) are much more effective change agents than nagging or scolding.

Think about it: Have you and your spouse ever experienced a major breakthrough because you stayed on them long enough that they caved and began doing things your way? Do you know any couple for whom the catalyst for life and joy in their relationship was chastisement? As Scripture says, "A soft answer turns away wrath, but a harsh word stirs up anger."[5] The most likely result of a knee-jerk, fleshly response is a downward spiral that will take the two of you even longer to recover from.

---

4. Ecclesiastes 4:9–10 NIV.
5. Proverbs 15:1.

So, choose grace.

Maybe this looks like giving your spouse some space, jumping in and taking a task off their plate, loving them in their love language,[6] or responding with gentleness rather than defensiveness. Whatever it looks like, choose to see your spouse's struggle as an opportunity to go on mission.

Let love cover a multitude of sins.[7] Move toward your spouse, praying to God in the moment for direction on how to love them well. Choose to put Jesus on display. Recognize your awesome privilege as your spouse's life partner to help in their sanctification. Point them to God as you love them unconditionally.

And give yourself grace. Remember that your struggle is not against your spouse. You are contending against the dark powers and principalities that seek to destroy you, your spouse, and your marriage for the way it reflects Christ's love for His church.[8]

Loving this way is countercultural, and probably counter-you. It's not natural to continue pursuing when you're offended. Getting used to the rescue mentality will take some practice. And we want you to know, we don't say any of this as people who nail it 100 percent of the time. Choosing grace still feels like a *choice* a lot of the time for us.

But we will say this: our conflicts are short-lived. Recently, we had a tough day. The next morning, we talked about it, we both laughed, and then we went on to have a great day together. Sin truly has no control over our marriage.

6. If you're not sure what we're referring to, see Gary Chapman, *The 5 Love Languages: The Secret to Love That Lasts* (Chicago: Northfield Publishing, 2015), and visit 5lovelanguages.com.
7. See 1 Peter 4:8; Proverbs 10:12.
8. See Ephesians 6:12; 5:32.

So, stick with it. Couples who fight to have a grace-based marriage are set on a solid foundation for growth, support, protection, and enjoyment.

WHAT GRACE IS *NOT*

It's important to talk here about what applying grace to your spouse and marriage *does not* and *should not* look like. The wrong idea about grace will not help your marriage thrive, nor will it reflect the love of God.

It Is Not Tolerating Ongoing, Egregious Sin

Most importantly, *grace* does not mean tolerating ongoing abuse, addiction, or infidelity. Enabling these sins by remaining silent or shrugging at them is not wise or biblical. To abuse a spouse or engage in extramarital sex and then demand your spouse's tolerance in the name of grace is disgusting.

Let's be clear—if you are abusing your spouse or being unfaithful, and you think you can do that with impunity because of the cross, you prove how little you understand grace. The gospel rings hollow for you.

Abuse, especially physical abuse, but also emotional and verbal abuse, is an affront to the tender heart of Jesus. He gave His life for His bride. He will never hurt her.

Infidelity shatters something sacred about the covenantal bond in marriage. It is an egregious insult to the wedding vows and to the faithful love of God.

If abuse or infidelity is currently occurring in your marriage, we urge you to prioritize your safety and seek professional help. A biblical counselor can help both of you sort through the devastation and vulnerability in your relationship. A good counselor can guide you and your spouse on a road to restoration, and he or she can apply God's truth to the delicate and painful parts of your hearts.

Your marriage is incredibly important to God, and He desires that it be renewed so that you can enjoy and display His faithfulness.

Grace Is Not Tolerating Manipulative or Controlling Behavior

Few people would defend physical abuse in marriage, but a relationship marked by one spouse controlling the other in any way is also problematic. In addition to emotional and verbal abuse mentioned above, some spouses engage in trying to control the other spiritually, financially, psychologically, and more.

Being gracious does not mean you are a doormat over which your spouse may run roughshod. That would be "cheap grace"[9]—the preaching of forgiveness without repentance, an attitude that justifies the sin without seeking the justification of the sinner, the idea that one should sin more so God's grace might abound. And cheap grace will doom a marriage as surely as it dooms a soul.

One couple nearly lost their marriage to this wrongheaded "grace." Steve and Anne had been married for over ten years when Anne announced that she had had enough and was

---

9. This phrase was made popular by Nazi-era pastor-turned-martyr Dietrich Bonhoeffer in his excellent book *The Cost of Discipleship* and echoes Paul's admonishment in Romans 6:1–4: "What shall we say then? Are we to continue in sin that grace may abound? By no means! How can we who died to sin still live in it? Do you not know that all of us who have been baptized into Christ Jesus were baptized into his death? We were buried therefore with him by baptism into death, in order that, just as Christ was raised from the dead by the glory of the Father, we too might walk in newness of life."

pursuing divorce. Steve was shocked. He told us he had thought their marriage was stable; he had zero complaints and hadn't heard any from her.

But Anne had been simmering for years. She felt controlled, like she could not be herself, as though she had to ask permission for everything and then was almost always denied. Believing it was the loving and dutiful thing to do, Anne had quietly tolerated Steve's domineering behavior. She acquiesced to all his financial and relational dictates. When the dam finally broke, Anne was overwhelmed by a torrent of hurt and resentment. She told us she could no longer trust her heart or any part of herself to this selfish, controlling man.

Steve was broken and confused. As Anne shared her feelings, Steve saw the truth in what she was saying. He listened, apologized, and asked for a chance to be a safer environment for her. Over time, Steve learned how to put Anne first and treat her as a true partner, and Anne slowly opened up to Steve. We're happy to report their marriage is intact and stronger now than it has ever been.

Cheap grace would have had Anne live in quiet misery for the remainder of their marriage. True grace won the day when she addressed the issue with her husband, then together they worked through it. Grace is usually costly—it was humbling for Steve to see his need for help and difficult to change bad habits. It was painful for Anne to seek help from others and allow God to soften her heart toward her husband. But grace was worth it—it was healing for both and saved their family.

If you are in a marriage with a controlling or domineering spouse and don't feel the freedom to address it with them, please seek a licensed Christian counselor for advice. You don't have to resign yourself to "it is what it is." Confronting your spouse with their sin in a safe environment may be some of the hardest, holiest work you do, and the reward is worth it.

Giving Grace Does Not Mean You're Giving a "Be a Jerk" License

One concern we sometimes hear from people who go to a Grace Marriage session basically amounts to, "Won't I be giving my spouse a 'jerk license' if I start loving them unconditionally? Won't I get taken advantage of if I respond graciously despite their bad behavior?"

We would wager you will not find this to be the case. With the above caveat that a pattern of controlling, manipulative behavior should be addressed instead of swept under the rug, most spouses will respond well to your choosing grace.

As Romans 2:4 says, "God's kindness is meant to lead us to repentance." Marilyn's grace and unconditional love motivate me to do better, not worse. The kinder and more gracious she is, the more I am drawn to her. The greater revelation I receive of the beauty of Christ, the more I want to abide in and worship Him.

The fact is, grace is attractive. Grace and love make better change agents than pressure and consequence.

A friend of mine would agree.

He admitted he tends to overwork, and his lateness—and missed dinners and bedtimes—had long been a point of contention with his wife. One night he was working late yet again, and let his wife know he would not be home for dinner. He got this text as a response from her: "No biggie. GRACE. Can't wait to see you when you get home!"

He told me, "I wanted to pack up my stuff and get home as quick as I could!"

The fact is, grace is attractive. As another friend once told me, "Whoever is kindest has the most influence." Grace and love make better change agents than pressure and consequence. And remember, when your spouse is short-tempered (or even downright nasty), it's probably not because they want to be. Few of us enjoy feeling angry or impatient. If your spouse is in Christ, Scripture says they are a new creation.[10] Deep down, they hate how weak they are in that moment. They don't want to live by the flesh; they want to live by the Spirit. Choosing a rescue mentality is very likely the fastest way to a restored spouse and happy home.

If your spouse does not know Jesus, then you have an incredible opportunity to live in such a way that they cannot deny the presence of God in your life. Your choosing grace can provoke them to godly jealousy; you can make them wonder what your secret is. Your tireless pursuit of your spouse even when they are unlovely is an excellent way they can be "won without a word."[11]

GRACE IS THE GOSPEL

This side of heaven, sin will remain in us. We will continue to fail God, our spouse, and others. The Bible acknowledges that those who marry will have many worldly troubles.[12] But God also uses marriage to make us more like Him. When we place our marriages under grace, the relational chasm created by sin

---

10. 2 Corinthians 5:17.
11. See 1 Peter 3:1–2.
12. 1 Corinthians 7:28.

is closed. Love covers a multitude of wrongs, and we become "ministers" of reconciliation. We become living, breathing agents of God's grace in the life of our spouse.

And the best news is, the way has been paved for us.

Jesus showed us extravagant grace when we did not deserve it, and the Holy Spirit empowers us to choose this same grace for our marriages when we call on His name. His unmerited favor and steadfast love are an endless source of living water for your soul, so you never have to pull from a well that's run dry. And nothing—no spouse, no situation, no history—is impossible for Him; He can be your very present help on even the hardest days.[13]

For those moments where grace feels hard—unseen, unappreciated, and ineffective—remember *this is the gospel*! You are living out a picture of the love of God. It *doesn't* seem fair sometimes to respond to sin with love, kindness, and grace. Yet this is precisely what Jesus did for us . . . and He tells us to love others as He has loved us.

When you're feeling out of steam, remember John 15:5: "I am the vine; you are the branches. If you remain in me and I in you, you will bear much fruit; apart from me you can do nothing" (NIV). There is no need to struggle to *achieve* grace or graciousness; that's the sneaky old performance mindset coming back. Rest in Christ. Abide in Him, in His Word. He will give you the grace you need, and your marriage will bear much fruit.

---

13. Philippians 4:13; Psalm 46:1.

DIGGING IN TO GRACE + INTENTIONALITY

What are a few common scenarios that tend to cause your spouse to struggle?

1.
2.
3.
4.
5.

When your spouse struggles or when you feel offended, what can you do to show love and grace? What is helpful to your spouse when he or she is struggling?

1.
2.
3.
4.
5.

4

Grace + Intentionality:

Sowing Generously to Reap Abundantly

The first big shift in our marriages means moving from a performance basis to a grace basis. We learn to grasp God's grace to us, and then extend it to our spouse—in every situation.

The second big shift means intentionality, applying God's Word to our marriages.

Scripture says that where your treasure is, there your heart will be, also,[1] and that as a man sows, so will he reap.[2] It further instructs us that those who sow sparingly will reap sparingly, and those who sow generously will reap generously.[3]

So, we need to ask ourselves: What kind of sowing am I doing for my marriage? Am I investing my resources—time,

---

1. Matthew 6:21.
2. Galatians 6:7.
3. 2 Corinthians 9:6.

money, creative energies, my heart—into my spouse? Or is he or she getting my leftovers?

Early on in our marriage, I (Brad) invested a lot of time, energy, and resources into my law practice. (Remember, I spent three hours a week bowling just to meet new people.) As a result, my law practice grew, and my clients liked me. But I invested little time, energy, or resources into Marilyn. And guess what? My marriage declined, and Marilyn didn't like me.

When I meet with couples in crisis, I'll instruct them to write down everything they are doing to intentionally invest in their marriage. Most of the time, they'll just look at me as if I had two heads. I'll say, "So . . . you aren't putting anything into your marriage, and you aren't getting anything out of it. I think we may be onto something."

Most of us would identify marriage as our most important horizontal relationship (our relationship with the Lord is often described as vertical). If that's true, we've got to act like it. How do we do that? With great intentionality, which we would break into two main categories: one is pursuit of your spouse, and the other is investment in your marriage.

PURSUIT: KNOWLEDGE + ACTION = LOVE

Intentional pursuit is central to the concept of grace. It is a natural outflow of your decision to lay down your life for your spouse.

This is, after all, why Christ went to the cross, and why He came to live among us in the first place. Jesus is God's pursuit of mankind, incarnate. The purpose of His life on earth was to reconcile us to God, to make a way for us to be with Him forever.

The formula for intentional pursuit goes like this: K + A = L. *Knowledge* plus *action* equals *love*.

Knowledge

Before you can love your spouse well, you need to *know* them. You can't hit the mark if you don't even know what the mark looks like. You have to be the world's leading SME (subject matter expert) on your spouse.

If we don't act with knowledge, our efforts can prove useless or even harmful. I once threw a surprise birthday party for Marilyn. We pulled up to a house full of her friends and a big sign on the door. I thought I had really hit this one out of the park. But . . . she hated every single minute of it and called it her worst birthday ever. Turns out, she is extremely uncomfortable being the center of attention.

I didn't act according to knowledge, so I didn't bless my wife. The only good thing that came from that birthday party is that I learned Marilyn does not like surprise parties!

Marilyn and I once counseled a husband and wife who were in crisis. The husband was completely befuddled as to why their relationship was in such a bad place. He listed, in great detail, all he did for his wife.

Then, we heard her perspective. She said he didn't do anything to love her. She felt lonely, unseen, and was ready to leave the relationship.

In working with them, we uncovered that this guy was, indeed, doing a lot of stuff for his wife, but he wasn't doing it according to *knowledge*. She felt loved when he spent time with her and when he gave her compliments or words of affirmation. He was not doing those things. He was, however, spending a lot of time serving her, and a lot of money buying her gifts. Yet none of that was communicating love to her. All his love shots were missing the mark.[4]

Once he started "learning" his wife, he could redirect his efforts to love her in ways she needed to be loved. He didn't have to work harder—the guy was really trying—he just had to work smarter. He needed to love her according to knowledge.

Two keys to loving your spouse according to knowledge are: (1) be a good listener, and (2) have a reliable strategy to retain information and ideas.

First, as the book of James encourages us, be quick to listen and slow to speak.[5] As your spouse talks, listen to what he or she says. Ask pointed questions to gain the most helpful information. For example:

Husband: "How are you doing today?"

Wife: "Not great."

Husband: "Why? What's wrong?"

Wife: "I didn't sleep well last night. I feel like life is so heavy and there is too much to do. I'm exhausted and feel like our house is out of control."

Using this information, the husband could then help clean the house and make sure they get to bed early that night. He could schedule a date to see a movie she has been wanting to see so she could check out for a few hours. She would feel heard, supported, understood, and loved.

You can also listen to what your spouse says even when they aren't talking to you.

---

4. See Gary Chapman, *The 5 Love Languages* (and 5lovelanguages.com). Dr. Chapman has discovered that we each have a primary love language, through which we feel loved: words of affirmation, acts of service, gifts, quality time, or physical touch.
5. See James 1:19.

Once we were in the Nashville airport, and I overheard Marilyn tell another woman, "I love your shoes!" When Marilyn walked away, I approached the woman and said, "I'm not trying to be weird, but where did you get those shoes?" I got the make and model, and those backless beauties were delivered to our front porch within a week. A short conversation, a quick internet order, and a memorable gesture of love.

Remembering details from past experiences can also help. For example, one time I (Marilyn) was leaving with our children on a short trip. Brad thought of our typical travel woes and tried to act on each one. He got movies ready for the kids, put phone chargers in the car, and put some of my favorite snacks and drinks in a cooler. It probably didn't take him long to do, but I felt considered and loved as I drove off.

None of this is rocket science, it just takes intentionality. If we listen to and are attentive to each other, with an eye toward action, our marriages can become examples of the love and creativity of Christ.

Second, take notes.

As you think of good gift ideas, potential dates, or solutions for recurring stresses on your spouse, write them down. Life has an uncanny way of erasing even our best ideas if we don't write them down.

We need a strategy to store and retain the knowledge we gain about each other. It could be a journal, a document or email draft on your laptop, or the notes app on your phone. You may even want to categorize them for easy retrieval. With thanks to Gary Chapman, we like to use his five love languages to categorize our note-keeping: (1) expressions of encouragement and gratitude, (2) gift ideas, (3) date ideas, (4) service ideas or projects, and (5) physical touch.

It's important to do what works for you, though. Get creative as you think of ways you can be a good student of your spouse.

Action

If you learn your spouse, but don't act on it, the knowledge is useless. The second part of pursuit is action. *Learn* your spouse, then *love* them accordingly. Sounds simple, right? Loving your spouse is why you signed up for this marriage gig. But we're talking about love as a verb, an ongoing action, not a feeling that comes and goes.

At first, I (Brad) got this all wrong.

Before we got married, acting on my love for Marilyn came naturally. Powerful emotion easily translated into talking on the phone for hours, holding hands in public, going on fun dates, giving kind notes and thoughtful gifts. But I got it wrong when I assumed all this would just organically continue once we got married. When the powerful emotion dwindled, so did the creative acts of love.

It takes *intentional* action to have a vibrant marriage. It takes *creating* fun and excitement to have a marriage that is fun and exciting. To love well, we must prioritize our marriage and take action. We've got to "marriage" like we dated.

When Marilyn and I started dating, I was nuts about her. I couldn't believe she was real. I would have done anything for her.

I even drove her to a date with another guy.

In my defense, this date was three hours away, and had been set up before I entered the picture. Marilyn and I were in Nashville at the time, and this guy was in Lexington, Kentucky. The way I saw it, if I got the first three hours and the last three hours of the date, Dude didn't stand a chance.

And I got that one right. Dude's not here today. I am.

Why? Because pursuit matters. It captures hearts. There was no doubt in Marilyn's mind when we were dating that she was my number one priority. But as I've said, that changed when we got married. I took my focus off her and turned to myself. I was consumed with my business, my wants, my feelings. I would have told you then that Marilyn was my most important human relationship, but she would have disagreed.

What would your spouse say?

I don't ask that to shame you. God never convicts us to condemn us. But He is zealous for His own glory and for the good of His children. If we are going to be proclaiming the power of Jesus in our lives, His power should be affecting all our relationships, especially our marriages.

If you're unsure where to start with pursuing your spouse, plan for it. Don't wait for your feelings to sweep you into action. Feelings tend to follow our footsteps.

Act in obedience first. Be strategic. Set reminders on your phone to text your spouse a word of encouragement every day. Ask God for wisdom in ways to love and respect your spouse better. Use your new note-keeping strategy to plan a date you know will thrill them. Study their love language and commit to loving them in the way they "hear" it best.

Maybe pursuit looks like a shovel in your hand at 5:30 on a random Sunday morning, as it did for me. Whatever it is that speaks love loudly and clearly to your spouse, make it your business to be about that.

INVESTMENT: PUTTING YOUR MONEY AND TIME
WHERE YOUR MOUTH IS

The second part of intentionality—sowing generously to enrich and grow your marriage—is *investment*.

This means investing your time and your money. This means taking Matthew 6:21 very seriously: "For where your treasure is, there your heart will be also." This means *dating your spouse*.

Date Your Spouse

A regular date night has been the second-most important thing we have done for our marriage, after gaining a new understanding of God's grace. Brad had a mentor who tried to sell him, rather aggressively, on the idea of a weekly date night for over a year. We initially resisted because it just didn't seem feasible, but finally gave it a try. Since then, we've gone on a date once a week (with very few exceptions) for over twenty-five years.

It's tempting to think of regular date nights as a luxury. Dating feels like a use of time that's neither practical nor financially prudent. But dating is *not* a luxury, nor a waste of time or money. Spending time together is a *necessity* for any healthy marriage. Everything needs care and attention to thrive. Your car needs regular maintenance, as does your personal health, the garden, and the dog. Your marriage is no different. You must invest in it consistently if it's going to grow and stay strong.

We get it, it's not easy. But it is worth it. Brad and I have had to work hard and get creative, but we have stuck to it. We are firm about this time together, and it has paid tremendous dividends.

We have continued through five kids, including a newborn with colic. Her screaming bouts were epic. One time Brad came home from work, and I was on one side of the house, crying, while Madeline was on the other side of the house, wailing. It was hard to keep a sitter, but we kept dating. There are still days where I am so tired, not a bone in my body wants to go on a date. And in hard seasons, I've been just about in tears before we even made it to the car. But we've kept dating. And it's been *so* worth it.

> **Quantity time makes for quality time.**

Early in our marriage, to get over the finances hurdle, we kept the dates cheap. We'd have coffee by the river or go on a hike. We traded out babysitting with friends so neither couple had to pay a sitter. Dating looks different through different seasons of life, but every week, we're sharing our hearts and sowing time alone together into our marriage.

Sometimes sticking to our date night is an unpopular choice with our kids or friends, but we are committed to it. As we often tell our children, one of the ways we can love them best is by loving and enjoying each other. And we remind them: they would prefer the regular date nights to regular arguing or to something happening to our marriage.

Don't get me wrong. Some of our dates are just bad dates. We have had dates where we were cold and distant the entire time.

In these times, it's been helpful for me to consider my relationship with Jesus. When I think on how I pursue the Lord, it shapes my perspective on dating Brad. I strive to be in God's Word and to pray every day, but not all my quiet times feel the same. Some days, I feel close to the Lord, like I'm learning so much. Other days, I feel distanced from Him, or walk away from a quiet time and immediately blow it with Brad or one of the kids. Likely you can relate to this. On bad days, it's easy to think my quiet time was a waste. But that's far from the truth. My consistent pursuit of the Lord over the long haul has grown my love for and deepened my relationship with Him. He has taught me and continues to teach me. He has changed me and is still changing me.

Dating your spouse will feel much the same. Sometimes your dates will be great, other times not so great. On some dates, you'll bicker and feel like it was a waste of time, but that is so far from the truth. If you faithfully date your spouse, you *will* see your relationship grow. Dating is a long-haul investment.

If you just can't pull off a weekly date, prioritize time together and try to get out at least every other week.

Because quantity time makes for quality time.

The more you make time for connection with your spouse, the more opportunities you create for those deeply meaningful conversations that leave you both feeling heard, loved, and excited for a future together.

You know what else makes for quality time?

No distractions.

Set these two rules for your dates. First, put the phones away. Leave the phone at home (or at least have the spouse who struggles most with the lure of the cellphone leave theirs if you need to stay accessible for the babysitter). Second, no one else is invited. Double dates don't count. You need time where you are solely focused on connecting with your spouse.

For us, it has also become a hard and fast rule that the date must be outside of our home. I can't relax in our house because it's too hard not to think of all that needs to be done. And our kids act like they're pigeons and we're fresh bread.

As to the date being weekly, it sure has worked for us, and we strongly recommend it. If you just can't pull it off, prioritize time together and try to get out at least every other week.

We realize that all situations are different; dating for one couple will look different from another. Many couples have additional challenges, such as children with special needs or parents who need care. The point is: make sure you are spending a lot of undistracted time together.

Find what works best for your marriage. Consistency is the key.

RETREAT ONCE A QUARTER

I (Brad) stole this idea from my time owning a law practice with my brother.

We realized about ten years in that we were never thinking about what we could be doing better because we were always bogged down in the daily to-dos. In addition to serving clients and managing hundreds of cases, we were consumed with payroll, human resources, and other administrative questions. We weren't growing because we were hamstrung by daily demands.

So, I attended a business coaching session in Chicago. One piece of advice I got there that transformed our law practice was this: every ninety days, get out of your business so you can focus on your business.

Once a quarter, take a retreat. Don't do any work *for* your business; just work *on* the business. Take a break from the day-to-day routine so you can cast vision, celebrate wins, address issues, and plan your next quarter. Take a break from the daily to make big-picture decisions.[6]

During the six years I attended those coaching sessions, our business took off. Our law practice grew from two lawyers to five, and from four staff to ten. Our income shot up, and my work week actually came down to less than forty hours. What happened as a result of these retreats was game-changing.

When I became the pastor to marriages at our local church, Marilyn and I thought, *Why wouldn't that idea work in marriage?* We started quarterly marriage coaching sessions with this model in mind. (This was how Grace Marriage got started.)

Every ninety days, couples spend time in marriage coaching together. They get an aerial view: What's working and what isn't? . . . What needs to change and how? . . . Where do we want to go? . . . What do we want our marriage to look like? . . . What's our team vision? They go through sessions and worksheets together, and then take time for each spouse to give uninterrupted feedback. They leave encouraged, heard, and with a plan for change where it is needed.

This same concept can greatly benefit your marriage too.

Once a quarter, get away from the routine and get an aerial view of your marriage. As the seasons of your marriage shift, assess together how you're doing. Make space for each spouse to share from the heart. Relax. Be refreshed by a break from the grind. Enjoy each other's company. Let time together and in the Word minister to your soul.

This recommendation always gets a little pushback, and I

---

6. With thanksgiving and credit to The Strategic Coach, Inc. (strategiccoach.com)

know it sounds like a lot. But trust us on this, a quarterly retreat with your spouse will do both you and your marriage a world of good.

It doesn't have to be lavish, and it doesn't have to be long. Even one night away can be helpful.

I would encourage you, though, to be firm on two points: no one else is invited (no kids, no friends), and you must get out of your house. Get away from all the daily stressors so you can genuinely focus on each other.

Our hope for you as you intentionally invest in each other is the same hope we've carried in our hearts since we founded Grace Marriage—that God would bring your marriage to life, that you and your spouse would richly enjoy each other, and that God's grand vision for marriage would be restored throughout our country and the world.

THE *WHY* BEHIND THE *HOW*

One reminder as we wrap up this chapter: this is *not* one more thing you need to do better.

None of the above encouragement toward intentionality in your marriage should feel like a burden. A self-willed initiative to go out and pursue and invest will exhaust your marriage, not rejuvenate it.

Remember the *why* behind the *how*. The reason you do this is the glory of God.

The purpose of intentionality is so much bigger than merely striving to have a good marriage. We offer each other grace and actively seek to love each other well *in order to put Jesus on display to the world.*

He loves radically, so we do too. He gives His life for His bride; we die to ourselves for the good of our spouse. We are pursuing and investing and dating to bring glory to God. Our marriages should bear witness to His joy, love, and grace.

And it is God's grace that empowers us to love, pursue, and invest as we ought. We don't do this in our own strength. Freely receive God's grace toward you. Meditate on His pursuit of you, His choosing you, His giving His very life to be with you. The more you receive from God, the more you will have to give to your spouse.

Refreshed and refreshing. Loved and loving. Forgiven and forgiving. Accepted and accepting. This is the rhythm of a marriage under grace.

DIGGING IN TO GRACE + INTENTIONALITY

List five fun times you remember having with your spouse.

1.

2.

3.

4.

5.

Which of these dates or experiences can you re-create and enjoy again?

1.

2.

3.

4.

5.

If you were to ask your spouse, "How could I love you better?" what would he or she likely say?

1.

2.

3.

4.

5.

What are a few ways you can regularly invest in your spouse and marriage?

1.

2.

3.

4.

5.

5

Grace and Identity:
Who Do You Think You Are?

Over the next several chapters, we'll talk about what a grace-based marriage looks like in different aspects of marriage, such as sex and communication, and in various seasons of life, like both crisis and the day-to-day. But before we do that, we need to talk about *you*.

A proper self-image is crucial to extending grace to others and to ourselves. If we don't understand who God says we are, we can't grasp the magnificence of His mercy toward us. If we don't see ourselves rightly, we won't process what others think and say about us in a healthy way. We can't walk in grace if we believe we are failing and perpetually feel pressure to do better.

WHO ARE YOU?

Who do you tell yourself you are? If someone could see inside your heart and could hear the way you talk to yourself, what would they report?

Perhaps you identify with the Exhausted Mom Who Isn't Doing Anything Well, the Man Who Doubts His Capacity to Succeed, the Wife Who Used to Be Interesting, the Guilt-Ridden Father, or the Aging and Unattractive Spouse.

When it comes to ourselves, many of us are harsh critics. But if you could see yourself as God sees you, you would be thrilled to introduce yourself.

Read the following paragraph aloud and let the Word of God wash over you as you hear who He says you are.

God claims me as His child; I am His precious son or daughter.[1] God calls me His friend.[2] I am an heir of God's kingdom, and a co-heir with Christ.[3] I belong to a chosen race, a royal priesthood, a holy nation, a people set apart for God's own possession.[4] I am a citizen of heaven.[5] I am free from any condemnation.[6] I am God's masterpiece, His handiwork, one He equipped for good work before the foundation of the world.[7] I am holy, blameless, and a saint in the eyes of God.[8]

If you are in Christ, *that* is who you are!

---

1. 1 John 3:1.
2. John 15:13.
3. Romans 8:17.
4. 1 Peter 2:9.
5. Philippians 3:20.
6. Romans 8:1.
7. Ephesians 2:10.
8. Ephesians 1:4; 2:19.

No matter the day or week you've had. No matter what others have said. No matter the lies you may be believing about yourself, that is your identity in the eyes of your Creator. And who God says you are is the truest thing about you. His Word is truer than your failures, your feelings, or even the facts about what you've said or done.

Not only are you of inestimable worth in His eyes, but He has commissioned you for the work of the kingdom.

A lot of us probably feel like God's primary emotion when He thinks of us is a sort of low-grade disappointment. He's always hoping for better from us; always let down when we do the wrong thing or make the wrong choice. We feel like He is quietly whispering, "Come on. You can do better."

But that's not true. He doesn't look on you with disappointment.

You are a new creation, sanctified, holy, a saint, and nothing—not even your mistakes—can separate you from the love of God in Christ Jesus.[9] He says you are the light and salt of the earth.[10] You are washed white as snow in the blood of the Lamb.[11] You bring Him exuberant joy; He rejoices over you with singing.[12]

Not only are you of inestimable worth in His eyes, but He has commissioned you for the work of the kingdom.

God's assignment to us from the beginning has been to rule over the earth, cultivate it, steward it for our good and His glory.[13] When Jesus ascended to heaven, He gave us a similar

---

9. Romans 8:38–39.
10. Matthew 5:13–14.
11. Isaiah 1:18.
12. Zephaniah 3:17.
13. Genesis 1:28.

charge: Go to the ends of the earth, cultivating souls and making disciples, that the name of God would spread throughout the world.[14] We are always, through the work of our hands and the words of our mouth, to be about the business of kingdom expansion. This is what we were made for.

We were *not* made to be downcast, insipid creatures, obsessing over our own morality. We were *not* fashioned in the heart of God for boredom, condemnation, and shame. We *were* made to push back darkness with light and bring order to chaos. We *were* made to bring the love and the very Spirit of God to every sphere we enter. This is what it means to be His royal children. This is the high calling that is ours.

THE SELF-GENERATED IDENTITY: FALSE AND FRUITLESS

Recently, I (Marilyn) was talking with one of our daughters. She shared how the thoughts in her head made her feel like a bad person. Like my daughter, many of us tend to equate who we are with our worst thoughts and actions. Yet God doesn't see us that way.

The enemy would have us be valued by our behavior. He would have us be preoccupied with our performance because this keeps our focus on self. As Major W. Ian Thomas puts it:

> The Devil does not mind whether you are an extrovert or an introvert, whether you succeed or whether you fail in the energy of the flesh, whether you are filled with self-pity or

---

14. Matthew 28:18–20.

self-praise, for he knows that in both cases you will be pre-occupied with yourself, not Christ. You will be "ego-centric" (self-centered) and not "Deo-centric" (God-centered)![15]

Satan doesn't care if you're wallowing in shame or puffed up with pride. It's a win for him if you're absorbed with all the ways you should be better. It's also a win if you're neglecting your relationship with Christ because you think you're doing pretty well. Either way, you're not focused on Jesus.

When our identity is self-generated rather than God-given, we will either defy or despair when we sin. We'll either defend ourselves and justify our sin or live in a sullen state of defeat. We cannot grow in holiness (or any of the fruit of the Spirit) from a position of frustration and shame. The "I failed yet again; I will try harder next time" mentality doesn't work.

More importantly, it doesn't align with the gospel.

The gospel says all believers are saved by the blood of God's only Son, are under grace, and can trust God to finish the work He started in us.

Did you hear that? The work *He* started in us. While we were still sinners, Christ died for us. In Christ, we have been given all we need for right standing before God.

The gospel is wonderfully humbling and magnificently encouraging at the same time. The way God sees us is not determined by how hard we work at being a good Christian. Our salvation is complete. Jesus, whose record is perfect, is both the author and *perfector*—that is, the starter and finisher—of our faith.[16]

---

15. Major W. Ian Thomas, *The Saving Life of Christ* (Grand Rapids: Zondervan, 1961), 86.
16. Hebrews 12:2.

FROM HEAVY TO LIGHT

It took me (Brad) many years to really get this. Intellectually, I knew I was a child of God, and my understanding of what Jesus accomplished on the cross was theologically sound. But I was still caught up in the performance mindset. I couldn't shake the feeling that the more I did for God, the more pleased He was with me. I was trying to "walk the walk," but I wasn't walking in His grace.

I was pushing myself more and more. I'd get up at 5:30 every morning to make sure I got in some reading, meditation, and prayer before the day began. I exercised each day, led a Bible study, and accepted invitations to sit on multiple nonprofit boards. I should have known I was climbing the wrong ladder when a woman in our Bible study told me, "I want to be a 'good Christian' like you."

You can bet that if I wasn't walking in grace toward myself, I wasn't walking in grace toward others either. Our marriage was hindered by my performance focus. Marilyn can tell you that before I learned to choose grace, our family's life and joy were stifled by my legalism.

I overanalyzed everything, trying to make sure we made all the right decisions. If she wanted to go out of town for the weekend with our family, we had to discuss in detail whether we were overcommitted. If she wanted to make a purchase, it sparked a long discussion on stewardship and generosity. It was as though every little thing had to be hyper-processed to make sure it was the best choice. As you can imagine, it really got on Marilyn's nerves. She gracefully endured what was probably many hours' worth of annoying biblical analyses and mini sermons.

My performance focus created a restrictive, law-based atmosphere, not one of grace and freedom.

After I was ordained as an elder, God brought me a mentor. I was cool with it because, hey, isn't part of being a "good Christian" having a mentor? Doug Hignell was well-educated and had a plateful of important things to do. He had his PhD, MBA, and engineering degree from Stanford. He owned a company with 180 employees. He had a wife and five adult children. He lived in California and was twenty-five years older than me. So, why did he choose to mentor a performaholic from Kentucky?

In Doug's words, "God told me to save you twenty-five years of trouble. I see myself in you. God freed me and told me to free you too." He saw my performance mindset like a name tag on my forehead, and aggressively sought to help me put it to death.

Doug helped me see that I was using the Bible as a self-help guide. He called me a moral narcissist. He pointed out that my moods, the rhythm of my days, how I treated my family, really *everything*, hinged on whether I had done what I thought I should do.

He asked questions about my time with God and showed me that it revolved around me. *What did I do well? What did I not do well? What do I need to do better?* The focus was on me, not on Jesus or others. Doug told me, "Your peace is based on your perception of *your* behavior, not on the perfect record of Jesus Christ."

At first, I resisted Doug's insight. It seemed to me that my mentor was pressuring me to stop doing good things. I told him, "I feel like if I listen to you, I'll be on my way down a dangerous and slippery slope!"

He shook his head: "You don't trust the Spirit."

What?!

He said, "If you mess up, do you believe the Holy Spirit will prompt you, teach you, and show you the way? Do you know what it sounds like to hear the still, small voice of the Spirit's conviction and guidance? Or are you too busy *doing* things to try to earn God's favor that you hear neither His delight in you nor His correction? Your problem is, you trust *you*, not God."

I continued to resist what Doug said until that day God broke my heart with the truth of His grace: "Brad, you're not okay, and that's okay. I am your Father; you are My son."

For the first time since I'd accepted Christ, I felt I could rest. I could cease my striving to be good enough for God. I realized in a fresh way that being a Christian is about Christ, not me. It's about taking Jesus at His word: "It *is* finished." Nothing more needs to be done.

> **Simply draw near to the God who loves you. Embrace the light burden, easy yoke, and rested soul He offers.**

A new understanding of the source of my worth—Christ's work, not mine—revolutionized every part of my life. Marilyn saw an instant change. When a friend asked her, "How did this new revelation of grace impact your marriage?" Marilyn's response was that it was as though everything went from heavy to light. Each little thing no longer had to be analyzed and scrutinized. Finally, we could just hang out and enjoy each other!

Don't get me wrong. I still have performaholic relapses, but the stress and anxiety of it is so miserable, I want to run back to grace as quickly as possible.

Perhaps you're like I was—driven, fatigued, frustrated, trying to be a better Christian. The answer for you is the same as it was for me. God didn't save you so you could go "full send" trying to impress Him. He saved you to enjoy Him and allow Him to work in and through you.

So simply draw near to the God who loves you. Embrace the light burden, easy yoke, and rested soul He offers. Receive the adoption He offers you. Trust in the perfection of Jesus for your salvation. Abide in His love and in His Word, and you will bear much fruit.

This is reason for both sincere humility and great confidence—you can't do it, but Jesus already has. Christ has clothed you with His righteousness, and you are now a child of light,[17] a royal jewel in God's hand,[18] the apple of His eye.[19]

SEEING RIGHTLY = LOVING WELL: IDENTITY AND YOUR MARRIAGE

A wonderful side effect of having a right view of ourselves is the way it changes our relationships with others. When you are no longer perpetually frustrated with yourself, you won't have to be frustrated with others, either. When you accept your true identity, people simply become easier to love. Sin is not held against you, and you don't hold it against others.

No longer are you trying to love messy Christians who need to fix their flaws. You find yourself enjoying and loving the adopted children of the King. You become gentle and

---

17. Ephesians 5:8.
18. Isaiah 62:3.
19. Zechariah 2:8.

others-focused instead of harsh and self-righteous. You become a Philippians 2 person: "Do nothing from selfish ambition or conceit, but in humility count others more significant than yourselves. Let each of you look not only to his own interests, but also to the interests of others" (vv. 3–4).

My mentor, Doug, once simplified the Christian walk this way: "Love the person in front of you and love them well."

When I visited him in California, I got to see him put this in action. He'd love the grocery worker, the coffee barista, and the waiter in a restaurant. It was like, wherever he went, the world stopped spinning as fast and the atmosphere changed. He brought kindness, slowdown, and grace to every place he entered.

At one point while we were eating lunch, an obviously drunk man walked up to our table and started talking. I was sitting there thinking, *I wish this drunk wasn't interrupting my time with Doug.* But Doug took a different approach. He turned to him, was kind, and asked him genuine questions.

As we were leaving, the guy came up to me, pointed at Doug and, with slurred speech, said, "I love it when that guy comes in. He is so nice."

Watching Doug love others well—treating each as a precious, unique creation of God—was incredibly convicting. I could feel the difference it made for those he met.

Each of us can love our spouse well in this same way—by affirming their true identity and regarding them as a son or daughter of God. You can bet that, if you have days when you think of yourself more highly than you ought, and perhaps even more days when you are discouraged about all that you're not, your spouse struggles in the same way.

Your spouse is an image bearer of the Most High God, just

like you. In *The Weight of Glory*, C. S. Lewis describes people's worth—and this includes your spouse—in a beautiful way:

> There are no *ordinary* people. You have never talked to a mere mortal. Nations, cultures, arts, civilisations—these are mortal, and their life is to ours as the life of a gnat. But it is immortals whom we joke with, work with, marry, snub, and exploit—immortal horrors or everlasting splendours. . . . Next to the Blessed Sacrament itself, your neighbour is the holiest object presented to your senses. If he is your Christian neighbour, he is holy in almost the same way, for in him also Christ *vere latitat*—the glorifier and the glorified, Glory Himself, is truly hidden.[20]

As an eternal being, made in the very image of God, your husband or wife is worthy of incredible honor. Wholly apart from all the good or bad things they do, your spouse is of eminent worth simply because they bear the stamp of the *imago Dei*. Your spouse is unlike any other created thing.

As a son or daughter of Christ, your spouse is a vessel of the Holy Spirit, a blood-bought child of the King of kings, just like you. Yet your spouse will struggle, just as you do, to comprehend and to rest in the remarkable truth of who they are.

This is where you come in.

God appointed you to be your spouse's life partner. When you think of kingdom work, you should think first of this man or this woman, the most important relationship God gave you to steward.

When their glasses get foggy and they start to lose sight

---

20. C. S. Lewis, *The Weight of Glory* (San Francisco: HarperOne, 2001), 46.

of who God says they are, help them see rightly. Encourage and affirm your husband or wife when you start to hear their negative self-talk. Be your spouse's chief helper against the onslaught of the world and the evil one.

When your spouse struggles in sin or makes mistakes, don't join with the accuser, who is always seeking to destroy. Let the words you say be God's words, rather than parroting the disparaging words of the devil. Affirm instead of condemning. Pursue instead of withdrawing. Choose grace and truth.

Step into your God-given role in your spouse's life and call forth their true identity. This may be some of the most important ministry you ever do.

LIVING OUR GOD-GIVEN IDENTITY AT HOME

How can we fight for a God-given identity to reign in our homes?

First, spend time with God—in His Word, in prayer, in worship, in a weekly Sabbath. Each of us is more susceptible to the lies of the enemy and the world's false narrative when we are not regularly washing our minds with the Word of God. We need to be reminded frequently of our worth in God's eyes, of who He says we are, and of our eternal destiny as citizens of heaven. See your time with God not as another box to check, but as a standing invitation to be refreshed, encouraged, and equipped.

Second, preach the gospel to yourself often. Remember, your hope is not in becoming better. Your hope is in God's grace, and this hope is secure. A bad day or a slip-up like raising your voice doesn't need to send you into an "I am the worst spouse/mom/dad" mindset. Remembering God's grace fosters worship and thankfulness for His forgiveness and power. Sin should lead you to repentance and confession, not to self-condemnation. Third, be careful how you speak to yourself and others. Words are powerful. If you tell yourself that you are unattractive and a failure, you are going to act like this is true. Similarly, watch your words and your tone with your spouse. We can build each other up or tear each other down with just a few words.[21]

Fourth, take care of yourself. When you need a break, take a break. If someone tries to help you with something, accept the blessing as a gift from God. Delegate some tasks to others. Enjoy your friends. Spend time developing hobbies, if possible. Schedule nights away as a couple to rest and regroup. Guard yourself against burnout and apathy so you are not susceptible to Satan's lies.

> *We are all works in progress, so extend grace to yourself and to your spouse. Show grace again and again and let even more grace silence the impulse to criticize.*

Fifth, serve others. One of the best ways to guard ourselves from falling off the other side of the horse is to regularly give of our time and resources to help others. This keeps us others-centric even when we don't want to be. Serve in at least one capacity at your local church. Disciple younger believers. Partner with local ministries in serving the disadvantaged and needy. Consider serving alongside your spouse in urban missions near your home, or even on an international mission trip.

Sixth, openly share your struggles with each other and with trusted friends. You need the support and insight of your husband or wife, and they need yours. Grace frees you to be authentic and

---

21. Proverbs 18:21a.

vulnerable. Your hope isn't in your performance, so you don't have to be self-conscious about how others view you.

We are all works in progress, so extend grace to yourself and to your spouse. Show grace again and again and let even more grace silence the impulse to criticize. If you or your spouse messes up, don't make a big deal of it.

Give each other breaks. Serve and date your spouse in such a way that there is no question as to how worthy and wonderful he or she is in your eyes. Love well. Ask God for wisdom in how to help your spouse walk in their true identity, and for grace to see yourself rightly too.

DIGGING IN TO GRACE + INTENTIONALITY

My mentor said the Christian walk can be distilled to this: "Love the person in front of you and love them well." How can you love your spouse more effectively?

1.

2.

3.

4.

5.

In what areas do you believe your spouse struggles to see themselves rightly?

1.

2.

3.

4.

5.

Specifically, how can you pray for your spouse?

1.

2.

3.

4.

5.

6

Grace and Expectations:
What Did You Expect?

L ike most love-hypnotized idealists, Marilyn and I didn't real-ize when we were engaged that we had wildly different ideas of what marriage would look like.

She imagined that we'd eat breakfast together each morning and discuss our hopes and plans for the day. In the evenings, we would eat dinner together and discuss what had happened that day. In our free time, I'd teach her to play tennis and we'd go on hikes. Life would be even better than when we were dating because we could be together all the time.

I imagined that married life would basically look the same as it did before, except now I'd have a beautiful girl by my side. She would be my constant companion; she'd do everything I did. She'd love coming to games with me. She'd love spending week-ends on the couch watching sports. She'd want to hang with me no matter what we were doing. And of course, we'd have a ton of fun with the new sexual liberties that come with being married.

Expectations then met reality, and the result wasn't pretty.

We never ate breakfast together. Marilyn would try to wake me up early, and I'd tell her, "You are worse than Memaw!" Now Memaw (my grandmother) was one of the finest people I've ever met, but when I visited her, she'd force me to wake up at 5:30 for breakfast.

Marilyn and I didn't go on walks. We never hiked or played tennis.

As for my expectations, she didn't come to games with me. She had no interest in sports. I was once in a tennis tournament just half a mile from our house, and she didn't come watch me play. But when I made it to the finals, I asked, "Are you coming to watch?" She said, "Do you want me to?" I said "Of course!" So she came. I won the match, but when I walked off the court, Marilyn asked, "Did you win? Everyone is so quiet in tennis, it's hard to tell who won."

Needless to say, she wasn't impressed.

She thought I was selfish, slovenly, and sports obsessed. I thought she was high-maintenance, critical, and way too sensitive.

MISMATCHED SUITCASES

Clashing expectations is a common experience in marriage.

It's as if each partner rolls up to the marriage table with a large suitcase. Each suitcase has three pockets. The first accommodates all the things other people have told them about love and marriage. This includes the unique dynamics of their families of origin, any mentorship, past relationships, marriage books, and so on. The second pocket contains each spouse's

ideas and interpretations of what God says about marriage
and husbands and wives. Finally, the third pocket holds each
spouse's personal ideas and convictions on what a husband or
wife *should* be like.

So, we all come to marriage with a suitcase stuffed full of "this-
is-how-I-should-behave and this-is-how-you-should-behave."
No two suitcases are packed the same way. It's like a couple
decided to go to Hawaii for a week. They're ecstatic; they can't
wait for the adventure. When they arrive, however, they realize
this is going to be trickier than they thought. He envisioned lots
of hiking, rock climbing, and a helicopter tour. She imagined
they'd lie on the beach during the day, do some snorkeling, and
eat at fancy restaurants at night. Neither one of them brought
the right clothes to do what the other wanted to do. Both, then,
need to make a few concessions and then get the right gear.
Both also need to change their mental picture of the vacation
if they are going to be happy.

This couple knew where they were going, but "Hawaii"
meant different things to each of them. If you are married, then
you, too, entered marriage with a suitcase full of expectations—
for yourself, your spouse, and your relationship. This is *totally*
normal. It's almost impossible *not* to have expectations for
something you haven't done before (like being married to
your particular spouse). But the problem is, our expectations
generally set us up for failure.

EXPECTATIONS KILL GRATITUDE

For one thing, expectations are the enemy of gratitude.
Take electricity, for example. We expect to have it, and we

don't even think about being thankful for it until it's gone. Recently, an ice storm knocked out our power for two weeks. When the power finally came back on, we were profoundly grateful for it . . . for about two days. Then we came to expect it, and our gratitude faded.

The same is true in marriage. When we start to expect something, we quit being thankful for it.

If your spouse was completely unhelpful, but then began proactively helping, you'd be grateful . . . until you became accustomed to the help. If your spouse worked too much and then scaled back, you'd be grateful . . . until you got used to their new hours. When good things become normal things, we typically forget they're something we used to hope and pray for.

Expectations can also keep us from seeing what is right in front of us. As a stark example, the religious leaders of Jesus' day expected a military hero to be their savior and ended up crucifying the true Messiah.

Likewise, we can miss the beauty of who our spouse is and their unique skill set if we insist on seeing them only through the lens of who we thought they'd be. But when we stop holding our spouse to the bar of our expectations, we are freed to be grateful for all they do. We have eyes to see the great gift from God that they are.

EXPECTATIONS BURDEN RELATIONSHIP

Think about your marriage for a moment. What is the main source of your arguments or struggles?

Typically, at the root of our uglier moments is a tangle of unmet expectations.

Maybe your worst arguments involve differing expectations on the Big 3—sex, money, and the kids. Or maybe you tend to clash about other things. But when you allow your expectations to rule your heart and dictate how you see your marriage, your spouse will usually be the problem. They will never measure up to all the standards in your mind. They will always fail.

The book of James addresses the reason behind relational discord. James basically tells us, "What causes fights between you? You want something and you don't get it."[1] You want certain behavior or certain things from your spouse, and they aren't giving it to you.

I (Marilyn) can certainly relate. For Brad and me, the root of some of our most memorable arguments has been money. Our definitions of "frugality" are quite different. Take grocery spending, for example. I prioritize healthy eating. Brad prioritizes staying within the budget and is often amazed at how much we spend on food every month.

A few years ago, he decided to "help" me grocery shop in a well-meaning attempt to get the bill down. He followed me around the store, lobbying for lesser priced items when I reached for my usual choices. He pointed out that the lunch meat I placed in the cart was three times the cost of what he picked out. I countered that his choice looked like a slimy bag of congealed chemicals.

Matters got worse when he offered, right then and there, to take over the grocery shopping for the family. I'm afraid my reaction was epic—like raised-voice-and-wagging-finger epic. I remember soundly rejecting his offer and adding, "We aren't going to feed our kids like they live in some frat house!"

---

1. See James 4:1–3.

As couples, we will have different perspectives and expectations as it relates to just about everything. And expectations make relationships less of a gift and more of a burden.

> As couples, we will have different perspectives and expectations as it relates to just about everything.

One husband in counseling told us about his mother. If he didn't call her, he'd hear about it. He once found this message on his voicemail: "I haven't heard from you in a while, but I wanted to let you know that I still love you." Every time she saw the grandkids, she'd say, "Wow, they have grown so much! They have totally changed since I saw them last." The message was clear: *I will put more and more pressure on you until you call me and spend more time with me.*

By the way, her approach did not have the desired impact.

Brad's grandmother took the opposite approach. Whenever he'd call her, she was thrilled. When she saw our family, she'd light up. She treated the visits and calls the same whether we had talked last week or three months ago. And guess what? We found ourselves *wanting* to call and see her.

One relationship felt like a duty; the other felt like a joy.

Grace and freedom are so much more effective than pressuring others to meet expectations. It's time to get rid of guilt and nitpicking and replace them with love and affirmation. It's time to release your marriage from the burden of expectations and grab hold of God's grace.

TWO CURES FOR OUR EXPECTATIONS

Expect to Find Your Ultimate Joy in Christ

It's simple, but true: Christ alone is the source of lasting, unshakable joy and hope. If you are often frustrated by the way your spouse is or isn't behaving, then you are likely expecting from them something only God can provide. As Gary Thomas says, "Much of the dissatisfaction we experience in marriage comes from expecting too much from it. . . . God didn't design marriage to compete with himself but to point us to himself."[2]

If you've gotten caught up in the mindset of asking your spouse to carry the load of needs only Christ can meet, you are not alone. This is tempting for all of us. But it is far better to bury those expectations and focus on how you are called to love your spouse, rather than focusing on how you want them to love you.

Let us challenge you to rethink the definition of marriage. It is a lifelong call to lay down your life for your spouse.

We cannot condition our love on our expectations being met. *If he is kind, we'll have a good sex life. If he gets short with me, I'll withhold. If she respects me, I'll engage and talk to her. If she nags me, I'll withdraw.* That is a performance mentality, not grace. That is behavior manipulation instead of gospel love.

Let's be crystal clear here—we are speaking of holding petty grievances against each other. As we said earlier, we do not mean to imply that any spouse should accept controlling, manipulative, or abusive behavior in the name of the gospel. We are talking about the tit-for-tat mentality that is so easy for us

---

2. Gary Thomas, *Sacred Marriage* (Grand Rapids: Zondervan, 2015), 27.

to slip into regarding daily annoyances and minor offenses.[3]

The best news is, turning to Christ is a win-win scenario. It points us in the direction of lasting satisfaction *and* takes undue pressure off our spouse. When you are seeking Jesus instead of your spouse's perfection, you are happy and whole because He promises to be found.[4] He is living water, a well that never runs dry.[5] And your spouse is released from a yoke they cannot bear up under. You are *both* freed to thrive and enjoy each other.

Cultivate Gratitude as an Act of Grace

We can further release our spouse from our expectations by cultivating the discipline of gratitude. We begin by realizing there's a difference between *reactive* and *proactive* gratitude.[6]

Reactive gratitude is circumstantial and instinctive. If someone knocked on your door and gave you five thousand dollars, you'd be grateful. If you got distracted and ran a red light with your kids in the car, narrowly missing a semitruck, you'd be grateful. This is reactive gratitude.

Proactive gratitude means looking for things to be grateful for. It looks for what is good in your spouse, kids, and friends and gives thanks for them. It sees blessing in every area of your life.

In our marriage discipleship, we like to call proactive gratitude being a "grace detective." It's a matter of tracking down the many good qualities your spouse possesses and thanking God for them. It's choosing to put their best attributes in the spotlight.

Thankfulness is not the default setting for many of us.

3. It is biblical and right to expect a marriage free from any form of abuse or infidelity. It is wrong to accept any of these things, if ongoing, in the name of love or grace. If abuse or infidelity is currently a part of your marriage, please prioritize your safety and seek help immediately from your local church or a licensed Christian counselor.
4. Jeremiah 29:13.
5. John 4:13–14; 7:37–39.
6. This concept and examples are from and attributed to The Strategic Coach, Inc. (strategiccoach.com)

For example, if your husband works hard, loves the kids, loves Jesus, and is not romantic, you'll likely think a lot about how unromantic he is. If your wife works hard, loves the kids, loves Jesus, and doesn't like to budget, you'll probably think a lot about how money should be spent differently.

Yet your marriage is not an exemption from Paul's charge in 1 Thessalonians 5:18: "Give thanks in all circumstances; for this is the will of God in Christ Jesus for you." Give thanks for the good gift you've been given in your spouse and extend grace in the areas that

Proactive gratitude is a gift that keeps on giving.

are lacking. Give thanks to God and give it out loud to your husband or wife, preferably in front of the kids and others, for all the wonderful things you see in them.

Proactive gratitude is a discipline; it needs to be developed. It is also a gift that keeps on giving. As Zig Ziglar is attributed with saying, "The more you are grateful for what you have, the more you will have to be grateful for."

It's true. The eyes of a thankful heart are trained to spot the good about who your spouse is and all they do well. Gratitude is the perfect antidote to our corrosive expectations.

YOU CAN STILL HAVE AN AWESOME MARRIAGE

We've learned that the key to strengthening your marriage is to focus on *your* growth, not on your spouse's. Focus on doing your part and leave your spouse to the Lord.

For example, if you feel your spouse lacks creativity and isn't pursuing you like you wish they would, *you* be the one to light the spark of fun, spontaneity, and intentionality. It's difficult for a marriage to stagnate if even one partner is infusing it with life and joy.

Gary Chapman tells a story that's a great example of this mindset. He writes that his wife always left drawers open, and it really got on his nerves:

> I did what I thought was the "adult" thing to do. I confronted her with my displeasure in the matter and asked for change. The next week, I observed carefully each time I entered our apartment, but to my dismay there was no change. Each time I saw an open drawer, I fumed. Sometimes I exploded.
>
> Then one day, I came home to discover that our eighteen-month-old daughter had fallen and cut the corner of her eye on the edge of an open drawer. [My wife] had taken her to the hospital. . . .
>
> She told me the whole story, and I contained my emotions while I listened. I was so proud of myself. I did not even mention the open drawer, but in my mind, I was thinking, "I bet she will close those drawers now!" I knew this would be the clincher. She had to change now![7]

But guess what?

Chapman's wife did not change. She continued to leave drawers open. Chapman says it was then he realized: *She is the drawer opener. I can be the drawer closer.*

When he extended grace and just decided to serve and help, it freed their marriage from ongoing, unnecessary frustration. The "drawer problem" that plagued their relationship and made

---

7. Gary Chapman, *The Marriage You've Always Wanted* (Chicago: Moody Publishers, 2021), 52–53.

him miserable was solved when he decided to be the solution. You, too, can choose grace. You can be the one to make your marriage better.

I (Brad) praise God that Marilyn wasn't content with a complacent coexistence early in our marriage. If she had resigned herself to unhappiness, it could have become the norm for our entire lives together. Even though she released me to the Lord, she continued to love me, pray for me, and pray with expectation for our marriage. It was some time before God broke me and our marriage took off, but Marilyn was content and joyful in the Lord even before I changed.

So don't get bogged down feeling sorry for yourself or assuming things will never change. Choose instead to make up for what is lacking in your spouse and celebrate their strengths.

Fix your eyes on Jesus; He is enough for your deepest needs. When we do this, when we leave our expectations for our spouse at the feet of Christ, we can find true fulfillment. We don't have to be dependent on another human for our happiness or meaning. We are freed to live joyfully and graciously because we are His and His Spirit dwells in us.

Remember: you don't love because your spouse first loved you, you love because *God* first loved you. And when we love each other unconditionally like this, we put the beautiful love of Christ on display for the world, to the glory of God.

DIGGING IN TO GRACE + INTENTIONALITY

What do you like about your spouse's:

Appearance?

1.
2.
3.
4.
5.

Personality?

1.
2.
3.
4.
5.

Character?

1.
2.
3.
4.
5.

Walk with the Lord?

1.

2.

3.

4.

5.

7

Grace in the Day-to-Day

Sometimes it is easier to extend grace during deep trials than in the day-to-day grind. During the hard times, whether family deaths or health crises, Marilyn and I have found it easy to cut each other some slack. We get closer when the going gets tough.

Great marriages are made not just in pulling together during the lows of hardship or the highs of celebration, but also in the flat days of doing laundry, packing lunches, and cleaning out closets. Many marriages unravel not because of a landmark fight or extreme difficulty, but because of the slow accumulation of resentment and distance that was never scrubbed away by grace.

God's grace is needed in the day-to-day moments because this is where we live most of our lives.

There are several reasons why the dailiness of life can be so hard on marriages, but personal differences and external pressures are two of the most significant. Let's address each issue and explore a few solutions to help us grow in everyday grace.

THE PROBLEM: PERSONAL DIFFERENCES

No two people are exactly alike, and this is a major source of friction in nearly every marriage.

No spouse behaves exactly like the other wishes they would. Priorities are different; tolerance levels are different. I once told Marilyn, "I bet you wish I came with a remote control!"

I'm guessing you could list some things your spouse does that drive you bonkers. Does she crunch her cereal loud enough to wake the dead? Do his gym clothes smell like a small animal died in the hamper? Does she always comment on your driving? Does he have an incredible capacity to tune you out?

Each of us has areas of weakness, sin patterns, and foibles that get on our spouse's nerves. And are you ready for the really bad news?

For most of us, those patterns rarely disappear entirely.

As I've said, I was messy when we first got married—like, college dorm messy. I'm now much better than I used to be, but without thinking, I'll still sometimes lay my sweaty workout clothes on the kitchen counter.

So, the key to harmony and peace can't be behavioral consistency. No matter how hard we try to appease our spouse, we are bent a certain way, for better or worse.

Solution 1: Grace in the Grind

The answer is an easygoing, everyday grace. Learn not to hold little annoyances against each other. Trust me, this is much more effective than trying to teach, train, motivate, or manipulate your spouse to be more like you want him or her to be.

I'll give you an example from our marriage.

I like lists, routines, and schedules. They are my path to productivity and peace. Marilyn hates them. She likes to go with the flow and get stuff done on her own time.

For a while, I tried to show her that my approach was more effective. I thought her productivity would skyrocket with a little coaching. But do you think she jumped on board with my checklists?

No. I got on her every nerve. She told me, "If I did life like you, I'd be absolutely miserable all the time!" Our debates over her way of doing life were never fruitful. But instead of expecting her to live like I would, I've learned to extend grace and allow her to be her. And she allows me to be me.

This can be hard to do.

Each of us thinks we are right. As Proverbs says, "Every way of a man is right in his own eyes."[1] Deep down, each of us thinks that if our spouse just bought into our program, life would be better.

One time, I (Marilyn) forgot to pick up a very important prescription for our daughter. By the time I remembered, the pharmacy was closed. I felt sick to my stomach. *How could I do that? She needs that medicine to prevent seizures! What kind of mom am I? There's no excuse for this.*

When Brad came home, I choked up as I told him how I'd blown it. I was prepared for a lecture on the importance of being more organized, of keeping lists so I didn't forget things like this. I certainly deserved it.

Instead, Brad hugged me tightly, then took my face in his hands and told me, "Marilyn, you do a thousand things every week. It is amazing you don't forget more than you do. I'll

---

1. Proverbs 21:2.

pick up the prescription on my way to work, then drop it off at school. And she'll be just fine. Don't worry about it."

What a tangible gift of God's grace! Brad's response set me free from feeling condemned as a terrible mom. If he had gone into lecture mode, I would have agreed with him. I might have even tried the list system (for a week or so). But that would not have benefited me; it would have increased the pressure I already felt and been unhelpful to our marriage.

Love covers a multitude of sins . . . and slip-ups.

Guilt and condemnation are poor building blocks for relationships. Love covers a multitude of sins . . . and slip-ups.

We counseled one struggling couple along these lines. We encouraged each of them to consider the other before themselves, and then apply grace when they felt offended. Discouraged, they looked at us and said, "That sounds hard."

"With all due respect," Brad replied, "what you are doing looks harder. Trying to lay down your preferences seems a lot easier than fighting all the time."

And it's true. It's easier to overlook offenses, love unconditionally, and serve than it is to live angry or be in a bad mood all the time. One requires some short-term pain, because dying to self always stings a little. But the other results in a lifetime of friction and distance.

Solution 2: Perspective: The Main Thing Is the Main Thing

Another important help for us in extending grace, day in and day out, is keeping things in perspective.

We needn't get bogged down in our spouse's humanity when we're focused on Christ's sufficiency. We don't tend to get hot and bothered over trifling offenses when we have eternal perspective.

Spend time with the Prince of Peace. Spend time at the foot of the cross. Preach the gospel to yourself daily. Read the Word. Saturate yourself in the knowledge of His love, greatness, power, and grace. Learn the things that are on God's heart and live accordingly.

Paul was speaking of much greater persecution than a frustrating spouse when he said, "This light momentary affliction is preparing for us an eternal weight of glory beyond all comparison, as we look not to the things that are seen but to the things that are unseen."[2] Keep heaven in your sights. Don't make your spouse's annoying tendencies into more than they actually are.

You are bought by the blood of Christ, loved beyond measure, and bound for endless glory. There aren't many bad moods that don't brighten when we're walking in that truth.

Solution 3: Go Positive Times Five

For many of us, our spouse's negative traits seem to take up too much of our brain space. When we think of our spouse, our mind may summon our frustrations faster than it remembers their good and pleasing attributes.

This negative bias is a well-documented psychological phenomenon. According to an article in *Psychology Today*, our brains react more strongly to negative things. There is greater electrical activity around negative news or thoughts than positive news or thoughts.[3]

This fact has huge ramifications for our marriages.

---

2. 2 Corinthians 4:17–18.
3. Hara Estroff Marano, "Our Brain's Negative Bias," *Psychology Today*, June 20, 2003 (last reviewed June 9, 2016), https://www.psychologytoday.com/us/articles/200306/our-brains-negative-bias.

Numerous studies show that positive thoughts about and interactions with our spouse must significantly outweigh negative thoughts and feelings—by a ratio of five to one—to overcome our natural negative bias.

The article cited above continues: "As long as there was five times as much positive feeling and interaction between husband and wife as there was negative, researchers found, the marriage was likely to be stable over time. In contrast, those couples who were heading for divorce were doing far too little on the positive side to compensate for the growing negativity between them."[4]

We can always choose the lens through which we see our spouse. We must train our minds to see each other through the positive lens of grace.

The Bible tells us in Philippians 4:8, "If there is any excellence, if there is anything worthy of praise, *think about these things.*" It might feel easier said than done, but we can overcome our inclination toward negativity. We can always choose the lens through which we see our spouse.

And we tend to find what we are looking for. If we look at our spouse through negative lenses, we'll find plenty of bad. But if we switch to positive lenses, we'll find plenty of good. We must train our minds to see each other through the positive lens of grace.

Fight the self-centered pull of negativity. Be a grace detective. Seek out the things praiseworthy about your spouse. Choose to view his or her traits as complements to your marriage instead of obstacles. Ask the Holy Spirit for help when

---

4. Ibid.

you are struggling. Seek to see and treasure the good gift you have in your spouse.

We promise you, the more you develop this practice, the more good things you will see.

THE PROBLEM: PRESSURES OF LIFE

Another source of discord in marriages is the fact that, on any given day, each spouse is under a great deal of pressure.

Day in and day out, husbands and wives must attend not only to their marriages, but also to work, the house, food preparation, the kids, and church and community activities and obligations. Life feels like a blur, trying to get it all done as quickly as possible so we can get to the next thing we need to do. We're stretched thin. Many days we feel we're doing all we can, and it still isn't enough.

It's no wonder, then, that when our spouse adds to the pile of pressure we're under with their moodiness or nagging, we often don't respond like we'd like to. We snap outwardly with a hostile response, or buckle inwardly, withdrawing into ourselves.

In bad cases, spouses are driven apart by the slow accumulation of discontent. In the worst cases, spouses turn elsewhere for validation and a fresh start—anything to get out of a marriage that feels like a yoke too heavy to bear.

But it doesn't have to be like that.

When we choose to help each other and prioritize our marriage over other demands, we'll find that the daily onslaught of stuff to be done doesn't need to sap the life from our marriages. Instead, it can be the catalyst for growing stronger and having more fun than ever.

Solution 1: Heed the Red Light on the Dash

One of the most helpful strategies Brad and I have found to help us choose a "rescue mentality" (see chapter 3) instead of taking offense is what we call the "red light on the dash." When your spouse is selfish, thoughtless, or snappy, think of it as a car displaying a "check engine" light on the instrument panel. His or her outward behavior is an indicator that something is wrong inside.

Imagine that Brad is short with me. At that moment, I have a few options. I could: ignore the problem and hope it goes away; get mad at him for it; or seek to remedy whatever has gone awry.

If I choose to ignore his struggle, things might get better temporarily. He might pull himself out of it and move on. But chances are, he'll be more susceptible to breaking down again . . . maybe soon. Ignoring a warning light on your car's display never fixes the problem and often results in a larger, more expensive repair. Likewise, ignoring your spouse's distress signals rarely resolves the problem.

Or I could get angry. I could verbalize my disappointment or offense and withdraw from him. But this is just as silly as yelling at your car for telling you something needs attention. It doesn't help the situation, and it doesn't help you.

Or I could be both smart and kind and seek to help him. I could choose to be part of the remedy.

So, when I notice Brad being withdrawn or snappy, I can choose to jump in and help him wherever he needs it. Likewise, when he hears me escalating with the kids or getting short with him, Brad thinks, *Marilyn's warning light is on*, and he does everything he can to help me get to a better place.

If you gently mention that you see they are struggling and

ask your spouse how you can help, they'll usually have an answer for you.

This concept has helped us become better friends and be a part of the answer instead of worsening the problem. It's an easy, practical way we can offer grace to each other.

Solution 2: Relationship > Productivity

The world praises us for getting things done. The more you seem to be juggling and accomplishing, the more accolades you'll hear. What you *won't* hear is anyone pushing you to spend more time with your spouse. To just hang out and enjoy each other.

We can all benefit from a gut check: Am I doing everything in my power to ensure my spouse knows how much I value them when I am away at work? Or when I am busy doing the things that "need" to be done? We all need encouragement to prioritize our key relationships over productivity. To create a marriage and family culture that is rich in relationship, you must be countercultural. The world around us values efficiency, effectiveness, and power. But God says, "Let *marriage* be held in honor among all"[5] . . . not you, nor your accomplishments.

Relationships don't give us a tangible sense of accomplishment, so they often take a backseat to things that do. However, Marilyn and I have learned that some incredible memories and relationship-building can happen when we create extra time for it.

When I decided to leave the practice of law and focus full-time on marriage ministry, Marilyn suggested we seize the opportunity to load the kids into the car and tour the country—for

---

5. Hebrews 13:4.

six months. This sounded a bit extreme to me, but the more we talked, the more I warmed to the idea.

Particularly, I saw the value in visiting Grace Marriage churches across the country that I may never have the chance to visit again. *This could be huge in getting our infant marriage ministry off the ground,* I thought. I made several calls, and soon I'd drawn up plans to visit a church, blogger, or radio station in every city where we planned to stop. "Rhoads on the Road"—it was going to be a hit. I informed the Grace Marriage board of our trip, and proudly rolled out my plans for how I was going to boost the ministry while doing this thing with my family.

My board responded quickly and bluntly: "No work for Grace Marriage on your trip, or no board for Grace Marriage when you get back." They were adamant that this was to be pure relationship-building. No work stress or distractions allowed.

How we have invested our time with Christ and with one another will determine the richness and longevity of our legacy.

So off we drove, leaving my laptop at home. I remember filling up the car with gas one August afternoon somewhere in southwest Texas, close to the Mexico border. Sweat was stinging my eyes. The kids were yelling at one another. Marilyn was calling out the window to please get something in the convenience store. The whole van stunk of dirty feet and leftover fast food. We had been on the road for one month, and I thought: *In two months, this will be halfway over.*

That trip was a monumental undertaking. Not all our moments were pretty, and some I'd prefer to forget. But words can't express how thankful I am for my board's advice. All the incredible memories we made and stories we have would have been squandered if I had sought to be productive instead of simply *being with* my people. My relationship with every single person in my family is different because of that time investment. I know not everyone has the luxury of being between jobs and able to invest *that* kind of time in their spouse and kids. It really was a once-in-a-lifetime deal. But I'd like to challenge the idea that just spending time with those you love isn't really doing anything. The greatest thing we can do with our time—and the *only* accomplishment that will matter on our deathbeds—is the depth of our relationships. How we have invested our time with Christ and with one another will determine the richness and longevity of our legacy.

This is especially true in marriage, as one couple we know discovered. Jason and Natalie were doing just fine—they didn't disagree often, were diligent parents to their four children, and were devoted to their marriage. But if you asked them if they really *enjoyed* marriage, they'd have to say no. The responsibilities of work and parenting took pretty much everything out of them.

When a Grace Marriage session at their church encouraged them to date and get away together on a regular basis, it felt like a revelation. Jason remembers asking himself, *Are we allowed to get away from our kids and just have fun together? Are we bad parents if we leave them to spend time with just the two of us?* He had never really considered the concept.

They decided to try it. For a full year, they tried to go on a date once a week and got away for one night each quarter. Jason says he felt like he was given a pass to enjoy his wife. They both say they are deeper in love with each other, are better parents, and have more fun in life because they started prioritizing spending time together. They've found that investment in your marriage is a *very* good investment.

We invite you to do a bit of self-assessment. Make a pie chart, assessing how you currently spend your time and energy. What percent of your week is devoted to enriching your marriage—after work, sleep, kids' stuff, activities, and other obligations?

Not much? Yeah, that used to be us, too.

But think about this: How you spend your time determines how you spend your life. How you spend your life determines who you are, and what you are about.

We want to be people who honor God in the way we love each other. We want to steward the gift of our marriage and our kids. We want our relationship to be a living advertisement for how a marriage under God's grace is fun, refreshing, and totally antithetical to the world's banal ideas.

We're guessing you want something like that for your marriage too. In both the small moments and the big choices then, make your marriage the priority it should be.

Miss out on banquets and games so you can keep your weekly date night. Turn down opportunities to be on boards or in social groups so you have more time for your family. Make eyes roll with your commitment to investing in your spouse.

It's worth it.

Kiss praise for your productivity goodbye in favor of something that really matters. Your care for the eternal soul of your husband or wife, your seeking to bring glory to God by the way you love them . . . these are the makings of a good and faithful servant.

This is the way to spend an everyday life that matters.

DIGGING IN TO GRACE + INTENTIONALITY

If you haven't already done so, draw a pie chart indicating how you spend an average day, including the amount of time you spend investing in your marriage. What needs to change, if anything?

How can you invest more time and energy in your marriage?

1.

2.

3.

4.

5.

What are some activities you need to scale back on to make time for your spouse?

1.

2.

3.

4.

5.

What are the warning signs that your spouse is struggling?

1.

2.

3.

4.

5.

List some helpful things you can do or say when your spouse's "check engine" light comes on.

1.

2.

3.

4.

5.

8

Grace in Crisis

A re you familiar with the children's song by Ann Omley about the wise man who built his house upon the rock?

A wise man built his house on a rock, and though the rains came down and the floods came up, the house on the rock stood firm. But a foolish man built his house upon the sand, and when those same rains and floods came, the house on the sand went . . . *splat!*

In marriage, it's not a question of *whether* the rains will come tumbling down and the floods will rise, it's a matter of *when.* And there's nothing like a crisis to show us if the foundation of our marriage is the rock of God's faithfulness or the shifting sands of circumstantial happiness. Will we stand firm? Or go *splat?*

CRISIS WILL COME

Jesus tells us that we will have trouble this side of eternity. "In the world you *will* have tribulation."[1] Life will not be easy. But

---

1. John 16:33

just before that, He encourages His disciples with these words: "In me you may have peace . . . take heart; I have overcome the world."

A friend of ours has experienced the depths of this truth.

Justin went out of town to attend his grandfather's funeral. His wife, Rebekah, stayed back with their children. On Sunday afternoon, Ezra, their two-month-old, took his afternoon nap. But when Rebekah went to wake him up, he wasn't breathing. He had passed away in his sleep.

No warning, no goodbye. Their child was just suddenly gone. Justin and Rebekah plunged into unimaginable grief. Rebekah said, "It was like the earth cracked open and darkness swallowed me up."

But their marriage didn't falter, as many do in this sort of circumstance. It thrived.

They point to three things that helped them grow closer through the loss: giving each other grace as they both struggled on the road to healing; sharing their hearts with each other— with all their grief, questions, and pain; and taking care of their marriage *prior* to the tragedy occurring.

Marilyn and I have walked through several seasons of crisis and difficulty in over twenty-six years of marriage, and I'm sure there will be more.

I bet you have too. And will.

When those storms come, we've found Justin's words to be true: "Even tragedy and hardship can be a time of growth in your marriage," he said, "if you choose to extend grace and share the process of healing with each other."

GIVE EACH OTHER GRACE

When our daughter Madeline was eleven years old, she came to sleep in our bed one night because she was having trouble falling asleep. Around midnight, Marilyn felt she should begin praying for her. At 2:00 a.m., Madeline began shaking violently and then stopped breathing.

I awoke to Marilyn screaming. As I ran around the house in the dark, trying to find Madeline's inhaler (and breaking our cordless phone *and* my toe in the process), I heard Marilyn cry that Madeline had gone limp. Sobbing, Marilyn held what we believed to be our dead daughter until paramedics arrived.

Madeline did revive, praise God, and we learned that she'd had a grand mal seizure. But doctors couldn't tell us what was wrong with her, or why it had happened, or that it wouldn't happen again. Furthermore, it would be a whole month until Madeline could get an appointment with a neurologist. One doctor tried to console us with, "It might never happen again, but just call 911 if it does."

As you might imagine, that was not comforting. Every night, I (Marilyn) slept in Madeline's room with her. I slept with my phone in hand, gripped with fear of her having another seizure. Each night as we got under the covers, my heart would start racing. I would pray out loud, with my heart pounding in my ears, pretending to be calm so our daughter wouldn't be scared.

Added to the trauma of Madeline's seizure, multiple doctor visits, and all the questions raised about her future were other burdens. We had a baby who still wasn't sleeping through the night. Another child had just been diagnosed with severe ADD. And recently, we'd found out one of our kids needed to be gluten- and dairy-free, so I needed to completely overhaul the way I cooked. I remember a trip to the grocery store during all this. I had no idea where to start. I didn't put anything in my cart. I walked every aisle and then went to the car and cried. I cried a lot that year.

I would go on runs by myself and cry out to God. I would try to hold it together in front of the kids, but anytime Brad and I left the house, I burst into tears. I cried on every single date we took. At night, I curled up in bed, dreading the next morning. I had no energy for intimacy or even laughter.

For a full year, I felt on the brink of a panic attack. I had absolutely no joy.

During this time, Brad could have lectured me, told me I needed to trust God more, told me I needed to be in the Word more. He could have told me how little attention I paid to him or his feelings, and how I could do better with the kids. And he would have been right on all fronts. But he did none of that. He just listened, helped where he could, and showed me grace.

Grace in crisis is not just a gift to your spouse. Grace in crisis is a lifeline, for your marriage and for your spouse's very soul.

God used time away at my parents' cabin to lift my spirits, and I remember realizing one day that I felt *happy*. I'd forgotten what that felt like.

On our next date, there were more tears, but these were tears of gratitude instead of grief. I thanked Brad for being patient and loving me when I had nothing to give back. I told him, "If you had told me to be more present with the kids, spend more time in the Bible, or show more interest in you, it would have crushed me. I was barely getting by. The grace you showed me was a balm that helped me heal."

This is how it goes in hard seasons.

Grace in crisis is not just a gift to your spouse, or a cherry on top. Grace in crisis is a lifeline, for your marriage and for your spouse's very soul.

No one in crisis is their best self; most of us are not even ourselves at all. We are broken and bleeding inside, consumed with pain, grief, doubts, and what-ifs. We are wrung out. We are numb. We have nothing to give.

What a gift of grace, then, is a spouse who comes alongside to help us carry our burden rather than adding to it. What a beautiful embodiment of Ecclesiastes 4:9–10: "Two are better than one, for when one falls, the other can lift them up" (paraphrased). God has given us to each other because we *need* each other. He has declared since the garden of Eden that it is not good for us to be alone.[2]

This is why it's so important—at all times, but especially in times of crisis—for us to choose a rescue mentality instead of taking offense. Choose to help and pursue. Don't pull away. Dig in and choose your spouse over yourself. This mindset will strengthen your marriage in any season, but in times of crisis, your pursuit may be the thing that keeps your spouse and your marriage afloat.

I (Brad) can attest to this.

I'll never forget the moment I lived a lawyer's worst nightmare. I was driving up a hill about a mile from our house when I felt a chill of fear and dread come over me. The thought hit me that I may have missed a deadline on a claim in a big case

---

2. Genesis 2:18.

for our firm. I rushed home, jumped on the computer, and my fears were confirmed. I was too late.

For the next several weeks, I struggled to sleep, and my mind raced day and night, looking for a way to remedy my error. I would frequently wake up around 3:30 a.m. and begin working because I knew there was no use trying to go back to sleep. I was in such bad shape that my staff said I looked gray; some of them even thought I might be seriously ill.

Desperate for relief, I tried to turn Philippians 4 into a peace formula. I gave thanks, made my requests, held up my hands, and waited for that "peace that surpasses all understanding" to hit me. The peace never came, but fear, misery, and anxiety kept pounding away.

I was distant. I was short. I was completely aloof to my family's wants and needs. I knew God's Word, and longed for His peace and comfort, but I couldn't find it.

Through all of this, Marilyn never took offense at my struggle.

When I came home from work one day, Marilyn greeted me and told me she was worried about me, that she'd been praying all afternoon that God would help me.

Thanks to a gracious client and an even more gracious God, the clouds lifted. A solution was found. I was eventually able to function and enjoy life again.

Despite my struggle, our marriage grew. Marilyn didn't pull back in hurt or disappointment even though I was certainly a disappointing husband at the time. She went to war for me. She went after me because *she loves me*, and she could do that because she knows how much *God loves her*.

That's the key to how this works. That's how we choose

grace when the roof caves in and we're left picking up the pieces of our life. That's how we become ministers of reconciliation when we have no strength in ourselves. That's how we have marriages that last "till death do us part."

We stand on the Rock. We remember who our God is, and what He says about us. We draw from His deep well of love and grace. Then we give away that which we've been given—freely and abundantly.

SHARE YOUR HEARTS; SHARE YOUR HOPE

In addition to giving each other the grace and space to fall apart during crisis, we must also keep our hearts and communication lines open toward each other. This allows us to share in the healing process and ultimately grow closer through trials.

Share Your Hearts

During the writing of this book, Marilyn's dad passed away unexpectedly.

It's difficult to put into words the profound effect Mr. Hudson had on both our lives, our family, and even on our ministry. He was always Marilyn's great champion; he delighted in her. They had breakfast together, just the two of them, almost every morning from Marilyn's eighth grade year through her senior year of high school. They were very, very close. I have a confident, sacrificial, and generous wife because of his investment in her.

You may remember that he was part of that marriage conference that grabbed my heart and shook me awake to all the ways I wasn't loving Marilyn as I should. He was zealous for our marriage, but not in a condemning way. During that time of awakening and repentance, he was never judgmental or harsh, but always encouraging and wise.

He was enthusiastic about Grace Marriage from day one. When he learned that I was thinking of abandoning a thriving law practice to start a marriage ministry, he was entirely supportive. In fact, his encouragement played a huge role in giving us the confidence to take the necessary step of faith. He didn't scold about supporting a family of seven on a sharply reduced budget. He saw kingdom ramifications and pushed us onward.

His loss continues to be a great heartache.

During this time of grief (and on some days it feels like we are still fumbling through it), Marilyn and I have found great comfort in sharing our pain with each other. We love to share memories about him. We laugh about things he said. We cry together too.

Sharing our hearts with each other helps us know we're not alone in our struggle. It also helps us know how we can best support each other. It keeps us close and helps us avoid emotional drift and isolation.

Talking this way makes for a good partnership. It acknowledges that you need your spouse and are trying to meet their needs as best as you can. When you keep communication lines open, you can show each other grace where it is needed most.

As marriage researcher Dr. John Gottman says, "Couples who make relationships work well adopt the motto that, 'If you're hurting, baby, the world stops, and I listen. I'm with you.'"[3] We deepen our bond by being there for each other. We don't just say we're teammates, we act like it.

---

3. Ellie Lisitsa, "Defensiveness: An Exclusive Interview with Drs. John & Julie Gottman," The Gottman Institute, February 26, 2014, https://www.gottman.com/blog/defensiveness-an-exclusive-interview-with-drs-john-julie-gottman/.

Good communication prevents offense from getting a foothold. When Marilyn lets me know she's struggling with grief or discouragement, I'm alerted to two things: First is that I need to go into high gear to be there for her. My partner needs me. And if she seems distant or moody, I don't need to take offense. This is not about me; Marilyn needs my support.

Share Your Hope

Sharing our hearts is one way we serve our marriage well in crisis; sharing the hope we have in Jesus is another.

In grief, as in all things, Christ is our example. In His darkest hour—the moments before His arrest and crucifixion—Christ was serving, encouraging, and praying for His disciples.[4] He knew they would be crushed and bewildered by His death. He equipped them for the coming upheaval by speaking truth to them: "You have sorrow now, but I will see you again, and your hearts will rejoice, and no one will take your joy from you."[5] And again: "Take heart; I have overcome the world."[6]

One of the most important ways we can love and help our spouse amidst crisis is to remind them of the truth about God and His sovereignty. Remind them that He has seen all things from the beginning; He is surprised by nothing. Remind them of the truth about their identity and security in Him.

Remind them, "It's Friday; it is only Friday. Sunday's a comin'!"[7]

We do not grieve as those without hope.[8] Though weeping

---

4. See John 13–17.
5. John 16:22.
6. John 16:33.
7. The text of this Easter meditation by S. M. Lockwood is available here: https://www.thegospelcoalition .org/blogs/justin-taylor/its-fridaybut-sundays-comin/. We highly recommend you do an internet or YouTube search for the original audio; hearing Lockwood preach it is particularly powerful.
8. 1 Thessalonians 4:13.

may last for the night, joy comes in the morning.[9] If the goodness and kindness and faithfulness of God's plan is not made manifest in this life, it will be in the next.

Grief, confusion, and heartache are very real. It would be dishonest to minimize the pain inherent to the human experience. But it would also be dishonest to let pain have the last word. The day is coming when we will walk by sight, not just by faith:

> He will dwell with them, and they will be his people, and God himself will be with them as their God. He will wipe away every tear from their eyes, and death shall be no more, neither shall there be mourning, nor crying, nor pain anymore, for the former things have passed away.[10]

Until that day, the words of Romans 8 are so comforting, which we quote at length because we need to be reminded of this when we are struggling:

> Now hope that is seen is not hope. For who hopes for what he sees? But if we hope for what we do not see, we wait for it with patience. Likewise the Spirit helps us in our weakness. For we do not know what to pray for as we ought, but the Spirit himself intercedes for us with groanings too deep for words. And he who searches hearts knows what is the mind of the Spirit, because the Spirit intercedes for the saints according to the will of God. And we know that for those who love God all things work together for good, for those who are called according to his purpose.

---

9. Psalm 30:5.
10. Revelation 21:3b–4.

What then shall we say to these things? If God is for us, who can be against us? He who did not spare his own Son but gave him up for us all, how will he not also with him graciously give us all things?[11]

We have a good Father. He is sympathetic to our weakness, frailty, and pain. His Spirit prays for us when we do not know how. And He who did not spare His own Son will surely give us the peace, the strength, the grace, and the mercy we need when we are hurting.

TEND TO YOUR MARRIAGE IN THE IN-BETWEEN TIMES

In giving me permission to share his story, Justin (my friend who lost his baby to SIDS) asked that I also encourage couples to invest in their marriages before the hard times come. He urged, "Tell them to take care of their marriages. If you are close, a crisis will only bring you closer."

Maybe it seems redundant to tell people reading a marriage book that working on your marriage is important, but it's true. The better the quality of your marriage before the storm, the better it will hold up during the storm. Our aim in this book is to convince you of the importance of your ongoing investment of grace in your marriage—as you build your house in day-to-day living, your relationship will stand in the troubles.

Studies on marriages surviving tragedy bear this out. For example, a 2003 study on parental bereavement published in the *Journal of Nursing Scholarship* noted that the quality of marriage

---

11. Romans 8:24b–28; 31–32.

prior to the child's death was a major factor in whether the marriage survived such a tremendous loss. Further, they found that tolerating a partner's grieving style (grace), keeping open lines of communication, and committing to stay married despite the stress of the crisis all contributed to marriage survival.[12] Give your spouse grace in the way they deal with any sorts of storms—loss of income, a move, serious problems with children, and so on—especially if their way of coping or grieving is different from yours.

Further, psychologists as early as the 1940s have been developing the "crisis theory" for longitudinal (long-term) marriage development and change.[13] These scientists create models and study why some marriages grow closer through trauma and others end in divorce. Crisis theory holds that the greater resources a couple has, and the closer their definitions for the shared tragedy, the greater the chances their marriage thrives instead of dissolves.

Put simply, marriages with storehouses of support, understanding, trust, and communication are best equipped to endure crises. Partners who know each other so intimately that they have a mutual understanding of the difficulties they walk through are much more likely to emerge hand in hand.

The weight of science and common experience compel us, we simply cannot wait until the going gets tough to get serious about working on our marriages. We pour into them now, with joy and intentionality. We invest in our marriages, considering

12. Stephanie Frogge, "The Myth of Divorce Following Death of a Child," *TAPS*, March 1, 2015, available at https://www.taps.org/articles/21-1/divorce.
13. Benjamin R. Karney and Thomas N. Bradbury, "The Longitudinal Course of Marital Quality and Stability: A Review of Theory, Method, and Research," *Psychological Bulletin* 118, no. 1 (1995): 3–34, https://www.healthymarriageinfo.org/wp-content/uploads/2017/12/The-Longitudinal-Course-of.pdf.

them precious and worth fighting for. We shore up our defenses not to avoid disaster, but to ensure we are victorious when disaster comes.

FIRM THROUGH THE FIRE

Crisis is undoubtedly a refining fire, both for our souls and our marriages. We are cast hard upon the Lord; any lack of faith we've been harboring will surface. We will learn who we really believe God is.

In marriage, the trauma of crisis burns away all the fluff and finery, and leaves just the two of us, raw and exposed. Any crutches supporting the marriage typically don't survive this fire. Some marriages collapse like a matchstick house.

But the good news is, the dross—the self-centeredness, pettiness, or lies we may be believing—doesn't survive, either. All that's left is the gold, the truth.

Our prayer is that your marriage is built on the rock of Christ, suited to withstand life's storms. We pray you are continually sowing seeds of kindness, generosity, and grace into your marriage so that the day-to-day is delightful, and hard times only serve to bring you closer.

DIGGING IN TO GRACE + INTENTIONALITY

Fill out the information below and share it, in detail, with your spouse.

The things that stress me most in life right now are:

1.

2.

3.

4.

5.

The primary emotions I am experiencing on a daily basis right now are:

1.

2.

3.

4.

5.

The things in my life that I wish were different are:

1.

2.

3.

4.

5.

Five things I think we could do to shore up our defenses as a couple are:

1.

2.

3.

4.

5.

9

Grace and Communication

Death and life are in the power of the tongue. (Proverbs 18:21)

W e don't think of our tongues as being performance-based, but they can be.

When I (Brad) worked as an attorney, I tried to be home by 5:30 to eat dinner with my family. But my ATA (actual time of arrival) usually lagged my ETA (estimated time of arrival), which became a source of frequent conflict with Marilyn. She would tell me, "When you have five kids, fifteen minutes matters. So, at the end of the day, don't organize your desk or chat with coworkers. Get home!"

It would drive her especially crazy when I'd pull up in the driveway and sit in the car on the phone for thirty minutes. I learned to stop doing that and just drive around the neighborhood until my work calls ended. Sometimes, I'd even park just around the corner to avoid being detected.

It seemed like a problem without a solution. I needed to return these calls—the speaker at my law school graduation had said it was the key to never getting sued—but my wife was more interested in me getting home on time.

THE PERFORMANCE-BASED TONGUE

So how could we break the end-of-workday conflict cycle?

Only by the grace of God, of course.

Marilyn took the first step. She decided she'd greet me warmly and speak to me the exact same way whether I got home early, on time, or late. She resolved to not let my timing dictate her mood. And her grace and love caused me to want to honor her more. I stopped lingering at work or in the driveway. I couldn't wait to get home and experience God's grace through her.

Can you imagine how different, "I'm so glad you're home; I've really missed you today!" felt from "Seriously? You couldn't just wrap that up after the kids went to bed?" The new response invited connection and promoted love. The old response created a divide.

It's important to note that both responses may have been honest. I think we can get tripped up by believing we have a right to express our feelings because we're just "being honest." Yet it's a gentle answer that turns away wrath, while a harsh response stirs up anger.[1] Marilyn's choosing kind words drew me closer and motivated me to consider her more than I had been.

We're not encouraging anyone to quash their feelings and

---

1. See Proverbs 15:1.

put on a big, plastic smile. Be open with your spouse about points of frustration when the timing is right and tempers are cool. It's a good thing to be genuine with each other and keep short accounts. But we must be careful that authenticity doesn't merge into self-indulgence. We are called to be peacemakers, be meek, consider others before ourselves, love one another with the self-sacrificial love of Christ. If an honest word can pass those tests, then it is good to share. If not, it's unlikely to please God or help our marriage.

AS GOES THE TONGUE, SO GOES THE MARRIAGE

The Bible recognizes the unique power of our words. It compares the tongue to many destructive things: a forest fire, a salty spring, deadly poison.

It also likens it to the rudder of a ship. Though small in comparison, a rudder can work against wind and waves to turn a ship weighing hundreds of thousands of tons. Where the rudder directs, the ship will go. Likewise, our tongues set the course for our lives and even our souls.[2]

With our mouths, we chart a course toward Christlikeness or toward destruction, for godliness or evil, for a marriage full of grace or one that feels like a war zone. This is sobering, but we should be encouraged. We can steer our marriage toward love, understanding, and kindness by *speaking* that way.

With such high stakes, how can we be sure the communication lines in our marriage ring with grace instead of condemnation?

---

2. See James 3:4–12.

FOUR KEYS TO GRACE-FILLED COMMUNICATION

Tend Your Soul

The most important thing you can do to create and sustain healthy communication in your marriage is to stay close to Jesus. Almost without exception, the closer you are to Him—the more time you spend in His Word, in prayer, and in seeking the things that are on His heart—the better your communication will be.

Matthew 12:34 says, "For the mouth speaks what the heart is full of" (NIV). You can think of your tongue as a spiritual diagnostic tool. What you say and how you say it reveals what's going on inside you. If your heart is full of grace, you will speak gracefully. If your heart is full of love, you will speak lovingly. If you have a servant's heart, your speech will be full of concern for others.

On the flip side, if your heart is full of anger, your speech will be harsh. If your heart is full of pride, you won't be open to others' input. If your heart is consumed with self, then your speech will be egocentric.

This is why James 1:26 says, "If anyone thinks he is religious and does not bridle his tongue but deceives his heart, this person's religion is worthless." If you believe you are close to God, yet your speech shows you are far from Him, then you are indeed far from Him.

And on a very practical level, especially in marriage, if you don't control your tongue, everything else you do is worthless.

If I work hard to please Marilyn—help her clean the house, help with the kids—and then I say some hurtful things to her, guess what? Nothing I did matters. She is hurt, and all my effort is gutted by my careless tongue. The problem is, taming the tongue is *hard*. James 3:8 even says it's impossible. If we're going to try to talk like Jesus would, we need supernatural help.

Tend to your soul before you seek to improve your communication. Speak with God before you speak your mind.

In His Word, our Father has promised to give us everything we need for life and godliness (2 Peter 1:3). We must be soaking in the Word regularly, washing our hearts and our minds with it, if we are going to have any hope of taming our tongues.

This is why we encourage you to tend to your soul before you seek to improve your communication. Speak with God before you speak your mind. Listen to the Holy Spirit before you ask your spouse to listen up. You need God's refining presence more than you need anything else.

Tune Your Ears

Good communication does require good sharing skills, to be sure. But mostly, it requires a whole lot of grace. And the most important way you can show grace to your spouse is by listening to what they say. What did they *actually* say? What are they trying to say? Why are they saying that? What are they not saying? Why are they using that tone or that decibel?

Each of these questions, when asked earnestly with a heart to understand, is a precious, selfless gift of grace to your marriage. Seek first to understand rather than to be understood, and you'll be surprised how quickly communication lines open.

Listening well sends a message: you are worthy of my time and attention. Listening tells the other person, "You are important to me. I really want to understand you and where you are coming from." This takes intentionality. It takes totally locking in on the person, giving them your undivided attention. Mostly, it takes listening with an ear to understand. Good listening is not planning your response while the other person is still speaking. It's waiting with a heart open to input, and a mind open to being changed or informed.

This is so important in marriage because when spouses get sideways, one or both feeling unheard is almost always a factor. When you don't listen well and just talk *at* your spouse, you prove that you are primarily interested in yourself. And, the Bible would add, you show yourself a fool. Scripture instructs us over and over on the importance of listening rather than speaking. Here's just a sampling from Proverbs:[3]

> Whoever guards his mouth preserves his life; he who opens
>   wide his lips comes to ruin.

> Whoever keeps his mouth and his tongue keeps himself out of
>   trouble.

> A fool takes no pleasure in understanding, but only in
>   expressing his opinion.

> Whoever restrains his words has knowledge.

> Even a fool who keeps silent is considered wise; when he
>   closes his lips, he is deemed intelligent.

> When words are many, transgression is not lacking, but who
>   ever restrains his lips is prudent.

---

3. In order, these verses are cited: Proverbs 13:3; 21:23; 18:2; 17:27a; 17:28; 10:19.

Ask yourself, *Am I a good listener? Do I give my spouse my undivided focus? Do I hold my tongue and really seek to know them?* Don't feel condemned if you have room to grow; we all do. But you can commit today to becoming a better listener. We have found it helpful to develop a few ground rules to foster good listening, including:[4]

- Refrain from doing other, "more productive" things while your spouse follows you around trying to talk to you. Maintain eye contact. Keep phones down when the two of you are talking.

- Catch yourself when your mind starts churning out rebuttals as they speak. Don't finish their sentences and rush the conversation. Don't hijack the topic they want to talk about.

- Don't top a tale. If they share a story, don't share another story on the same subject. If they say, "Ugh, I had a hard day," just learn everything you can about their day. Don't jump in with how hard your day was.

- Summarize what you've heard. For example, when Brad is finished sharing something significant with me, I'll say, "So, what I am hearing you say is ____." It's funny how he can say something, and I won't hear him right or get it *at all*. But this practice of playing back what I heard allows misunderstandings to be cleared up quickly. And, most importantly, it shows him that I was really listening and seeking to understand.

It's simple, but true—when people feel listened to, they feel loved. They feel valued, secure in the relationship, and safe to

---

4. These ideas are from the teaching of Brian Crall.

open up and share from the heart. This unlocks a tremendous door to deeper, meaningful conversation.

Take It Deeper

In many marriages, communication can feel more like a business transaction than intimate relating—*Here's the plan for the day. Here's the plan for the weekend. Please take the kids here. Please pick this up on the way home. How was the meeting? How was work? Good, good.*

Couples are often too distracted or uninterested to have heart-level conversations. As a result, shallow talk becomes the norm.

So, how do we foster a culture of deep conversation? Two big requirements here: become a good listener (which we've covered) and make a practice of sharing your heart.

Talking on a heart level with each other is a *huge* component of good communication in marriage. It allows you to know your spouse and be known by them. It helps each of you feel truly seen, heard, and loved. It prevents cracks in the relationship from becoming canyons.

It guards against some other man or woman becoming your spouse's confidant.

In short, deep conversations deepen the roots of a relationship.

For some of us, though, it's just not natural to talk about emotions or what's in our hearts. This is the case with me (Brad). I can talk and talk to anyone, but I typically stay away from anything deep or emotional. I wholeheartedly believe in the importance of it, I'm just not naturally good at it.

One time I got incredibly angry at another attorney who had, through deceit, gained the upper hand in a case. I was ticked. I spewed like a fire hydrant—colorfully and not very Christianly—to Marilyn about it. Her response was surprising. When I finished, she said, "I loved that." She didn't condone all the things I said, but she really appreciated my sharing my deep feelings with her.

Marilyn wants to know what I'm thinking and how I am doing. She wants to know me and feel close to me. So, when my emotions aren't so raw, I've made a real effort to share with her what I am feeling.

This was hard at first. What helped me get in the habit of sharing deeper things was journaling. After writing

> *Try to take phrases like "I'm fine," "I'm good," "It's okay," "It went well," and "It's all good" out of your vocabulary.*

about my concerns, I could reference it or read it to Marilyn to help her stay connected with me. That may sound crazy to you, but it helped me get through a mental roadblock when it came to talking about what was going on inside.

Also, I had to intentionally be more detailed in my responses to her questions. If you struggle with this, as I have, try to take phrases like "I'm fine," "I'm good," "It's okay," "It went well," and "It's all good" out of your vocabulary. Summary avoidance statements like these are barriers to connection. Instead, slow down and share the details of the experience or emotion.

Marilyn says this was a big win for our relationship. When she knew I was struggling with something, she knew not to take my bad attitude personally. When she knew I needed help, she wanted to come alongside me.

If I withdraw and isolate, Marilyn is more likely to take offense. But if I tell her when I walk in, "Today was a really hard day; I'm so frustrated," she sympathizes and realizes my struggles have nothing to do with her or our relationship.

Sharing our hearts with each other keeps us close, helps us in our struggles, and increases our intimacy. Our marriage can be rich even when—spiritually, emotionally, or physically—we are each very "poor" (that is, when we are hurting, down, and needy).

For heart-sharing to happen, though, you have to be a safe "place."

Be a Safe Place to Share

We have spotted two ways we can unwittingly thwart our spouse's attempts to have a heart-level exchange.

The first is by intercepting or stunting a would-be deep conversation because it feels uncomfortable to us. For example, if your spouse says, "I feel like I am failing as a parent," you want to quickly negate that thought and tell your spouse what a great parent he or she is. Yet good communication means listening and seeking to understand first. Why does your spouse feel this way? How often? How can you help? There is certainly a place for encouragement but *understanding* needs to come first.

We all have a friend who we refrain from sharing our fears and difficult questions with because we already know what they'll say. They'll gloss over our vulnerability with a wave of their hand and a quick verbal Band-Aid.

Let's not be that friend, especially for our spouse. Let's be the one they run to with all the hard things they are thinking and feeling because they know we will unequivocally listen to, understand, and affirm them.

The second way we keep communication shallow is by

trying to correct our spouse's perspective. Unfortunately, we have a great example of this one.

We shared in an earlier chapter about our eldest daughter's grand mal seizure when she was eleven. In the wake of the initial crisis, she needed multiple tests to determine the cause. The days and weeks of labs and scans and waiting on results were incredibly stressful. We were both very scared.

On the day we met with the doctor to receive the results and a diagnosis, he came in and told us, "The tests are all normal. Her brain looks great."

This was an unbelievable relief—at least to me (Brad). We got in the car afterward, and Marilyn asked, "How do you think the appointment went?"

"It went great!" I answered, beaming. "He said her brain looked normal! How do you think it went?"

"Awful," she said quietly. "Something is terribly wrong, and we don't know what it is."

I lost my patience. After all the worry and tests and prayers, we had gotten the answer we wanted. Right? Marilyn's anxiety was preventing her from being grateful for what I felt was a gift from God. "What do you mean it was awful? This is exactly what we prayed for! What do you want, an abnormal brain? A tumor?"

I didn't seek to understand her. I just tried to convert her to my point of view.

You might guess the effect this had on Marilyn's heart.

I (Marilyn) retreated into myself. I was scared, hurt, and angry.

The tests the neurologist ran had been traumatic. These tests had sought to bring on irregular brain activity so they could locate which part of Madeline's brain was causing the seizure. This involved flashing lights in her face, keeping her up all night to cause sleep deprivation, and forcing her to a point in exercise where she couldn't catch her breath. Watching her go through this, and watching for signs of another seizure, had been terrifying.

We had gone through all of this only to hear the results were inconclusive.

All Brad had seemed to hear was that her brain scan was clear, that there was no tumor. But I fixated on the other things the doctor had said: "It's hard to catch brain spikes with seizures; unless it happens again, we are not going to do anything at this time. Keep an eye out for things that can bring on seizures, like stress, sleep deprivation (she loves to stay up late), exercise (she runs cross-country and track), and flashing lights. Don't let her take baths. Stay close by when she swims, and if she is in a lake, make sure she wears a life jacket. If it happens again, we'll run more tests."

While Brad was relieved and grateful that there was no bad news, my mind was spinning with what-ifs. Nothing felt safe for Madeline now.

Our differing perspectives were compounded by our different personalities. Ever the extrovert, Brad processes his point of view out loud, so I kept hearing him share the "good news" we got with others. All the while, my introverted self was processing my concerns internally, and I grew distant. *Did Brad not even hear the doctor? I guess all the things we need to watch for are on me because he doesn't even think anything is wrong. Must be nice to feel so good about something so hard.* These thoughts didn't lend themselves to great feelings toward Brad, and he got annoyed by my melancholy. His attempts to talk me into graciousness only made matters worse.

After a week of icy distance between us, Brad made the first move toward working things out. "Why were you so discouraged by the appointment?"

I let him in on some of my deep-seated fears. "They told us they don't know what triggered this, and they don't know whether it might happen again. Something is wrong with our daughter, and we don't know what it is! We have no assurance that it's fixable. I worry about whether she's getting enough sleep. I worry that she's exercising too much. I worry as her mom that I might do something that could trigger it. I worry that I might wake up to find she's had another seizure—or worse—while I slept. I live in fear all the time."

When I (Brad) finally listened, Marilyn's perspective made sense.

If I'd sought to understand her answer instead of correcting it, I could have saved us from a week of rocky relationship and been a supportive husband when she really needed one.

Lesson learned.

If you crave heart-level communication with your spouse, you need to be a "place" where their thoughts and fears can land without debate. Don't shut them down or make them go on the defensive just because you don't understand them. *Listen.* Ask clarifying questions, if necessary. Seek to understand the "whys" and "hows" of their feelings. Affirm your care for them.

This is the way to deeper communication that leaves you both feeling seen, known, and loved. This is the way to rich, meaningful conversation that is a vessel of God's grace in your marriage.

IT'S OKAY TO NEED HELP

Maybe all of this sounds simple enough, but it's not working for you. Maybe the topic of good communication in marriage is painful.

If you have sincerely tried to implement the principles we've presented in this chapter, and you just can't seem to communicate on a deeper level with your spouse without distance or argument, please see a licensed Christian counselor. A third party who is skilled in navigating relational complexities and operates under the umbrella of Scripture can be a tremendous help to you.

An inability to communicate may feel dyed-in-the-wool from families of origin, or stem from crises or other sources that feel insurmountable. In a godly counselor, your marriage will have an advocate who can help you remove roadblocks and open lines of heart-level communication.

We opened this chapter with "death and life are in the power of the tongue." The Bible also says, "The mouth of the righteous is a fountain of life."[5] May our homes overflow with life, joy, and love as we seek to grow in godliness and grace through our communication.

---

5. Proverbs 10:11.

DIGGING IN TO GRACE + INTENTIONALITY

Highlight or underline the communication tip below that you most need to work on.

Focus more on listening than on talking.

Make sure you are sharing your heart and emotions with your spouse.

Maintain eye contact.

Give your spouse your undivided attention.

Don't hijack topics.

Don't top a tale.

Practice summarizing what you have heard.

What are your spouse's interests? What are they most passionate about?

1.

2.

3.

4.

5.

How can you prioritize these interests and steer conversation toward these topics to enhance your friendship and communication?

What are the dominant worries and stressors in your spouse's life right now?

1.

2.

3.

4.

5.

When and how can you seek to understand your spouse better in his or her areas of worry and stress?

1.

2.

3.

4.

5.

10

Grace and Criticism

I n the previous chapter, we talked about grace-filled communication in marriage, which basically looks a lot like a freshly
paved four-lane highway. Traffic flows safely and smoothly in
both directions. There is good giving and good receiving. Each
spouse gives the other attentive ears and gracious words, and
receives input with an open, sincere heart.

When communication includes criticism, the traffic pattern
should look the same.

THE MEASURE OF A MARRIAGE'S MATURITY

A mentor once told me (Brad), "If you want to measure a
man's spiritual maturity, watch how he responds when criti-
cized or rebuked."

These are true words about people. They are also true words
about marriages.

Scripture is clear: the wise embrace rebuke; those who get
angry and defensive are stupid (or mockers or fools). These
are God's words, not ours. Examples include:

Whoever loves discipline loves knowledge, but he who hates reproof is stupid.[1]

Whoever corrects a mocker invites insults.[2]

Do not rebuke mockers or they will hate you; rebuke the wise and they will love you.[3]

Fools show their annoyance at once, but the prudent overlook an insult.[4]

If a marriage is rich in spiritual maturity and grounded in the Word of God, both spouses can hear criticism humbly and will ultimately grow closer. But where such maturity is lacking, criticism brings conflict, bitterness, and division.

Negative reactions to criticism are understandable. Who likes to hear they're wrong or are performing below expectations? We feel our hackles raise when someone starts pointing out things we don't want to see.

Then how do we fight the knee-jerk reaction to put up walls or launch a counteroffensive when our spouse brings an area of needed improvement to our attention?

You guessed it—grace.

Grace in criticism looks like listening and learning, limiting the critical things you say, and keeping the endgame in mind.

LISTEN AND LEARN

The first key to keeping your marriage under grace when the conversation trends toward criticism is to shut your mouth,

1. Proverbs 12:1.
2. Proverbs 9:7a NIV.
3. Proverbs 9:8 NIV.
4. Proverbs 12:16 NIV.

listen to your spouse, and consider where you may have been wrong or have something to learn.

This is tough. When you *want* to talk the most, it's probably time to talk the least. Frustration-fueled words send your communication into the ditch. But listening instead of reacting has tremendous benefits. It de-escalates the situation, leaves room for the Holy Spirit to correct either or both of you, and gives you an opportunity to grow.

Take a common scenario in our marriage as an example. Marilyn values a clean house. My default mode is messy. This difference has provided me with plenty of practice in accepting criticism. Usually without thinking, I do something that triggers a conversation that starts with, "Brad, would you please?!"

Before I learned to communicate better, my response was basically, "You just don't see how hard *I* work! Do the trash cans roll themselves up the hill? Does the bed make itself?"

And how do you think she responded to that?

She stopped, reflected, realized what a loving and hardworking husband she had, and apologized to me. Right?

Uh . . . no. She arrived at the same conclusion she had so many times before: *This is never going to get better.*

Not long ago, we entered the criticism cycle once again. This time, the trigger was my leaving my shoes in the middle of the floor. After tripping over them on her way to the bathroom she said, "I feel like you just add more work to be done around the house and don't help carry the load."

Thankfully, I have grown in grace during the course of our marriage. This time, I responded differently: "Why do you feel that way?"

"You don't help with the laundry. You don't empty the dishwasher; you don't even put your own dishes *in* the dishwasher. You leave a trail everywhere you go." And she listed a few other areas where I was not giving her the help she needed.

This time, I listened first and then told her I would really make an effort to help more. Later that day, I did a few loads of laundry, helped with the dishes, and asked her if she needed anything else before I relaxed after dinner.

The next morning, Marilyn hugged me and said, "I'm sorry I came down on you so hard yesterday. I was harsh and spoke from frustration. I'm really sorry."

> If someone only tells you things you want to hear, they aren't loving you well.

When she retold this story to a group she was teaching, Marilyn emphasized that my response kept our conflict from escalating. If I had taken offense at her criticism and sought to invalidate her position, she would have been even more frustrated. A gracious response and practical help left her to deal with herself and to be convicted by the Lord of a critical spirit.

By listening instead of defending myself, I helped Marilyn and our marriage.

And, let's be honest, I helped myself too.

Many times (more times than we'd like to admit), we need to hear the criticism our spouse brings to us. This is why we listen and *learn*; each of us has plenty to learn from the person who knows us the best.

"As iron sharpens iron, so one person sharpens another."[5] Each of us has blind spots. We *need* our spouse to help us see

5. Proverbs 27:17 NIV.

what we don't see on our own. We shouldn't resent the gift they are to us as a living, breathing mirror that shows us where we have room for growth.

This is what Scripture means when it says, "Faithful are the wounds of a friend."[6] If someone only tells you things you want to hear, they aren't loving you well. If your spouse is a faithful friend, they *will* speak into areas of sin and needed growth in your life. Your spouse is one of the greatest instruments of sanctification God has given you.

If listening and learning is not yet your instinctive reaction when your spouse brings you critical feedback, here's a cheat sheet to help you get in the habit:

Pray. We both love the prayer of David in Psalm 139:23–24: "Search me, O God, and know my heart! Try me and know my thoughts! And see if there be any grievous way in me, and lead me in the way everlasting!" If you are consistently praying like this, it's a good bet that your spouse won't need to approach you with sensitive matters very often, and your heart will be in a good place when they do.

Resist getting defensive. Defensiveness derails conversations. Proverbs 21:2 says, "A person may think their own ways are right, but the LORD weighs the heart" (NIV). Let those words be a warning; don't try to prove yourself. Listen and seek to understand your spouse's perspective.

6. Proverbs 27:6.

Don't throw punches. It's human nature to come out swinging when we feel cornered. Don't change the subject by throwing your spouse's failings in their face.

Ask if you heard it right. Each of us has filters through which we listen to others, so it's essential to verify that we're hearing correctly.

Say thank you. This is counterintuitive, but if your spouse didn't care about you and your marriage, they wouldn't bother with this discussion.

Proverbs 15:32 says, "Whoever ignores instruction despises himself, but he who listens to reproof gains intelligence." While criticism isn't pleasant, it might be exactly what you need. Listen and receive criticism graciously from your spouse. When you do, you'll play a key role in growing your marriage's maturity and keeping the communication lanes open.

FEW AND FAR BETWEEN

It is important to learn to *accept* criticism. But it is also important to *limit* criticism.

Very little fruit comes from spouse-to-spouse criticism. (And none comes from behind-their-back criticism.) Neither of us can recall ever hearing anyone say, "The primary thing God has used to grow me is my spouse's daily input and critique." In fact, Scripture compares a nagging spouse to living in the corner of a roof or in a desert.[7] Ongoing criticism is also

---

7. See Proverbs 21:9, 19.

likened to the constant dripping on a rainy day.[8]

Conversely, Proverbs 17:9 says, "Whoever covers an offense seeks love." You want your marriage to overflow with love, peace, and intimacy? Choose grace and gratitude over complaining and critique.

Trust the Holy Spirit to work on your spouse's heart. You are an instrument in God's hand to help shape your spouse, but you are not responsible for their growth. Only God can do that.

When Brad and I were engaged, his mother told me, "Brad runs at either two hundred percent or zero." She was right; he's either hyper-focused or he has checked out. He gets a lot accomplished—or not much at all. He's overflowing with joy and cheer, or he's grouchy. This often takes a little adjustment from my perspective. Sometimes I get frustrated and point out that he's in a mood . . . which usually goes over about as well as yelling at someone stuck in a ditch, "Hey, you're in a ditch. Get out!" It's not helpful.

Recently, Brad invited me to read his prayer journal. As I read it, I realized he knows when he's struggling. He had written all the things he hates that he does when he's frustrated or in a bad mood, and asked God for help with them. Hearing his heart gave me so much compassion for him. I felt convicted by the Lord to shut my mouth when he's struggling and pray for him. Pray for wisdom on how to love him well and help. Let the Holy Spirit grow and mature Brad; that's not my job.

The truth is, most of us know where we are weak. We all want to do well and are aware of our failings. So, all of us need a lot more encouragement and affirmation than critique.

For one thing, affirmation is a far more powerful motivator

---

8. See Proverbs 19:13.

than criticism. An atmosphere of encouragement is the healthi-
est way to live in unity and under grace with your spouse. When
we accuse and criticize, we unwittingly align ourselves with the
enemy, who "accuses [the saints] day
and night before our God."[9]

We tend to find what we are looking for. If we look for the bad, we'll find plenty. If we look for the good, we'll find that instead.

Don't hear us say never give each
other input. There must always be a
place for that. But let critical feedback be the exception, not the rule.

If you'll get in the habit of seeking
each other's input, you will find that
to be a much better starting point for
conversations on where each of you can improve. Your spouse
knows you better than anyone else, and their differing perspectives can be so helpful. So, *proactively* seek each other's input;
don't *reactively* complain about each other's faults.

Remember that we tend to find what we are looking for. If
we look for the bad, we'll find plenty. If we look for the good,
we'll find that instead.

One time, I allowed my feelings toward Brad to get stuck
in a negative rut. For days, I mulled over all the things he did
wrong, until one morning I told him, "Even the way you're
drinking coffee right now is getting on my nerves!" Realizing
that I was in a bad place, I spent some quiet time with God,
prayed, and wrote down a bunch of things I loved about him
as a way of changing my feelings. By the end of the day, I truly
liked him again!

It takes discipline to train our minds to focus on the positive.
We tend to dwell on what bothers us and take for granted all

---

9. Revelation 12:10.

that is going well. When we choose the negative, we create an opening for the devil to drive a wedge between us. However, when we choose to focus on the good and excellent things about our spouse, we glorify the Father and strengthen our marriage. We "give thanks in all circumstances," which "is the will of God in Christ Jesus for you."[10]

Cultivate this discipline. Choose to view your spouse's traits as complements to your marriage instead of obstacles. Ask the Holy Spirit for help when you are struggling. Seek to see and treasure the positive qualities in your spouse. The more you develop this practice, the more things you will see.

PLAY THE LONG GAME

So much of the time when conflict or criticism gets a couple at odds with each other, they seem to forget that they're on the same team. Nobody wins by crushing their own teammate. Teammates win or lose together. So, when you spend a ton of emotional and physical energy "winning" the argument or convincing your spouse they were wrong, you both lose. Repeat: you *both* lose.

A quote attributed to Hank Smith goes like this: "Placing blame in marriage is like saying, 'Your side of the boat is sinking.'"

It doesn't make sense. So, whether listening to criticism or looking to dole it out, remember you're on the same team. It doesn't matter who is right. What matters is that both of you love each other well and are right before God.

---

10. 1 Thessalonians 5:18.

Let this be a gut check when criticism starts to cause conflict. We have friends who use a simple phrase to cool things down when tempers begin to flare: "Hey, I'm on your team." Another thing couples often forget in the heat of the moment is that the goal is to look like Christ. He showed us what it looks like to live a life in the center of God's will. He was also the humblest man to ever walk the planet. He "did not count equality with God a thing to be grasped, but emptied himself, by taking the form of a servant, being born in the likeness of men."[11] Your spouse's criticism can actually help you grow in Christlikeness if you let it. Even if they are on your case in an unhelpful way, you can still exercise the muscles of patience, self-control, and considering others before yourself. You can make small decisions that shape you, bit by bit, into the image of Jesus.

Perhaps you'd like to tell us that your spouse can be quite terrible. But do you know who was ridiculed, reviled, called names, and lied about?

Jesus.

And do you know what He did about it?

He laid His life down for the offenders and prayed for them—as He was dying *for them.*

Fix your eyes on Christ next time you're tempted to feel sorry for yourself because of your nagging wife or overbearing husband. His grace knows no bounds, and it is certainly sufficient for you.

Remember that your spouse is not your enemy. But your marriage does have a very real enemy, and his goal every day is to turn you against each other. He would love to see you tear your home apart from within.

---

11. Philippians 2:6b–7.

Marriage is a covenant relationship, so play the long game. Don't get bogged down in petty offenses and allow pride to push you away from your spouse. Resist the devil's schemes to destroy your marriage. Claim God's grace over you both. Allow criticism to bring you even closer together. Be a team. God will get much glory as you grow in love, understanding, and maturity, and your marriage will greatly benefit.

DIGGING IN TO GRACE + INTENTIONALITY

The Criticism Scale

Self-awareness is a necessary step toward growth and maturity. Rate yourself on how well you receive input and criticism.

Receiving Criticism

Based on the descriptions given below, circle the number that best represents your overall response to criticism.

1——2——3——4——5——6——7——8——9——10

Defensive and closed

Receptive and open

Ready with a counterattack

Willing to keep listening

Make excuses

Take it to heart

Giving Criticism

Based on the descriptions given below, circle the number that best represents your overall approach to offering criticism.

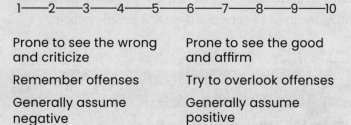

1—2—3—4—5—6—7—8—9—10

Prone to see the wrong and criticize	Prone to see the good and affirm
Remember offenses	Try to overlook offenses
Generally assume negative	Generally assume positive

How can you grow in both giving and receiving criticism?

1.

2.

3.

4.

5.

What are some ways you can promote an atmosphere of affirmation in your home and marriage?

1.

2.

3.

4.

5.

11

Grace and Sex

Our guess is, when you scanned the table of contents and noted a chapter on sex, you had one of two reactions: "Yes!" or "Ugh." Sex is not something many people feel ambivalent about.

Most married couples have some sort of struggle over sex. When counselors talk about "The Big 3" that cause conflict in marriage, sex is the one with the blinking, neon sign. It's the one everyone wants to, or needs to, or is scared to, talk about.

And it's no wonder.

Sex is uniquely powerful. It can unite two souls and bring both lovers indescribable joy. It can also be the ruin of marriages, legacies, public figures, and empires. It is a fire that can warm your whole house when kindled and kept appropriately. And it can burn the whole thing down in an instant when squandered.[1]

Sex has such great power, for good and for evil, that we want to acknowledge from the get-go: this chapter is important but

---

1. This illustration is borrowed from Ray Ortlund.

may be uncomfortable or simply not the right word at the right time for some. With the prevalence of sexual abuse and difficult sexual pasts, the breakdown of the family, and the cultural normalization of pornography, complicated issues surrounding married sex have now become more of the norm than the exception. If this describes you or your marriage, we strongly encourage you to seek professional help to work toward healing and progress. While we are big fans of sex within marriage (for the reasons we'll get into below), we want to emphasize that it is not a silver bullet—it is not a cure for porn addiction, emotional disconnection, or brokenness. Where there has been a breach of trust, that trust must be rebuilt. Where there has been a wrong view of sex, that view needs to be renewed. And the spouse who has broken trust or sinned against the other sexually may need to give their husband or wife time to heal, with sex off the table until that point.

Further, we recognize that some couples have mental or physical limitations preventing them from regular sex—or even having sex at all. We pray such couples experience no condemnation in this chapter. Instead, we pray you and your spouse draw closer together as you share your hearts and struggles.

MARRIAGE'S SWISS ARMY KNIFE

The crux of this chapter is this: sex is even more important for your marriage than you think it is. Sex is your marriage's Swiss army knife—it is useful in multiple ways, supporting, defending, unifying, and bringing life to your relationship.

Great sex requires great grace, and great sex is an act of great grace. Regular, mutually delightful sex is a hallmark of any grace-based marriage.[2] Let's see why this is so.

SEX IS FOUNDATIONAL

Sexual intimacy was created by God for His glory, and it was His idea that sex be an integral part of marriage. Genesis 2:24 states a command of God as He surveyed the newly created first man and first woman: "They shall become one flesh." Don't miss that. Sex was part of God's plan for marriage in Eden. In other words, when God was drawing up plans for the perfect marriage in a sinless world, sex was a part of that plan. And sex has certainly been part of His plan for marriage ever since.

Paul restates God's decree to become one flesh in Ephesians 5:32, and goes on to say, "This mystery is profound, and I am saying that it refers to Christ and the church." The sexual union between husband and wife is analogized as a picture of Christ's future union with His bride, the church. Even so, the holy, mysterious, timeless significance of sex is often lost on us.

Life happens, and we start to view sex as less of a foundation and more like shrubbery. It's superfluous, it's easily replaceable, and we don't even notice it's ailing until it's too late.

Unless a couple intentionally pursues a healthy sex life, external stressors can extinguish marital intimacy. With the

---

2. There are, of course, always exceptions to every rule. Sex is difficult or even impossible for some marriages because of health complications or physical disability. We do not mean to imply that, for these marriages, the grace inhabiting their marriage is less than whole. For the most part, however, we have found that many people believe their marriage is an exception to the idea that sex is important when it is *not*. If you can have sex, you should, and with regularity.

realities of daily responsibilities and frustrations, fatigue, and physical changes, it may be rare that both a husband and wife are filled with sexual desire at the same time. And when they only come together when both are in the mood, sexual connection is infrequent at best.

The world doesn't help us here, either. The popular view of sex strips it of its power and potency and cheapens it to a commodity. Sex is something magazines, movies, and other indicators of culture promote as a skill that should be honed with many partners. It is just a physical act to be perfected for one's own prowess and selfish pleasure.

The self-centered view of sex that the world peddles will devastate our marriages if we let it. We should know that the Hollywood scenario of two desirous lovers frantically ripping each other's clothes off isn't reality. Yet it's tempting to start believing that *that* is what sex should be like . . . and if it isn't, you're being ripped off.

This sexual performance mindset misses the point of God's design. Sex should deepen your connection to your spouse. It shouldn't be an obligation they need to fulfill for you; it is an opportunity for you to serve them in a way no one else can. Sex should not be about what your spouse can do for you, but how you can bless and love your spouse.

Sex should be about mutual selflessness. Sex should be a way we live out Christ's example.

Infrequent sex or selfish, one-sided sex is like a hairline fracture in a marriage's foundation. A lack of real intimacy brings emotional and spiritual instability. This insecurity creates distance, leaving all kinds of room for wrong thinking about each other and about sex.

Over time, what began as a small fracture can widen into a dangerous chasm. The result can be deepening feelings of isolation, relational disconnection, emotional or physical infidelity, or an overwhelming struggle with lust. In addition, many families, even in Christian homes, have been infected by the lure of pornography.[3]

> **Perhaps the thought hasn't occurred to you that spiritual forces seek to prevent you and your spouse from having great sex.**

These things should not be!

We believe Satan actively seeks to prevent married couples from a robust and regular sex life because he knows it serves to strengthen their marriages. You can be sure, if God designed and delights in marriage, Satan hates it and seeks to destroy it.

Perhaps the thought hasn't occurred to you that spiritual forces seek to prevent you and your spouse from having great sex. Perhaps you just feel like it's age or busyness or stress that saps you of your desire for each other.

But the spiritual struggle over our sex lives is real.

We cannot be caught off guard here. We must join the fight. With intentionality and prayer, we can start a sexual revolution in our homes and throughout the country, with sex being seen as the rich blessing and powerful protection that it is.

SEX IS BONDING

Sex is also important for your marriage because it is uniquely designed to knit the two of you together. God declared that

---

3. Sixty-four percent of Christian men and 15 percent of Christian women say they watch pornography at least once a month according to Covenant Eyes, Pornography Statistics, 2018; available at https://www.covenanteyes.com/pornstats/.

you should become one with your spouse. Pause a moment and take inventory of all the things that tend to keep you and your spouse apart:

schedules and busyness
children
jobs (or the loss thereof)
health issues (illness, anxiety, depression)
pregnancy
bills and financial responsibilities
arguments
chores or housework
endless entertainment options

You can probably think of more. The point is that God, in His infinite wisdom, gave us something that serves as a glue when our life circumstances are trying to tear us away from each other. He imagined, designed, and blessed the physical union of a husband and wife. He did this because He knows this physical bond connects us in deep ways.

In the Bible, we can see that when God thinks of sex, He thinks of a union that goes much deeper than our bodies. When Genesis 4:1 says that "Adam *knew* Eve his wife," something more than the act of intercourse was being described. The same word (in the Hebrew language) appears in other places in the Bible to describe knowledge, understanding, and personal regard—all of which are nonsexual yet intimate ways of relating.

Sex is *not* just physical; it's a deep knowing of souls. And God designed it to be that way.

Research shows that it's not just an emotional glue that is

created when we have sex, but a chemical one as well. The primary hormones and neurotransmitters released during sex are oxytocin and dopamine, both of which attract us to each other, activate our brain's reward center, and help us bond.[4] One author says this about the benefits of these hormones:

> Sexual attraction and sexual arousal bring to bear two very important hormones, dopamine and oxytocin, both of which create bliss and bonding. Even if the lovemaking session started out with only a modest amount of interest, once arousal starts, these hormones create attachment, pleasure, and intimacy. . . . Frequent sex is a great bonus and even an essential part of most couples' commitment and happiness with one another.[5]

If sex was God's idea, and He gave it to us to glue us together, shouldn't we strive to mutually enjoy this gift with thanksgiving and regularity?

But note that we said, *mutually* enjoy.

It's important to remember that the health of a sex life is not necessarily measured by the frequency of sex. All the bonding benefits that can be part of sexual connection evaporate if one spouse isn't being considerate of the other. If one spouse is selfish, demanding, and thoughtless, that one-sided sex can be worse than no sex at all. In some cases, it becomes actual abuse.

Let the exhortation of Romans 12:10 be a metric for the health of your sex life: "Outdo one another in showing honor."

---

4. Katherine Wu, "Love, Actually: The Science behind Lust, Attraction, and Companionship," *Science in the News* (blog), February 14, 2017, http://sitn.hms.harvard.edu/2017/02/14.

5. Suzanne Wright, "Can 365 Nights of Sex Bolster a Marriage?," quoting Peter Schwartz, PhD, available at https://www.cbsnews.com/news/can-365-nights-of-sex-bolster-a-marriage/.

When you seek to love your spouse in your lovemaking, God's design for blissful, bonding sex can have its full effect.

SEX IS PROTECTIVE

Sex also preserves and protects your marriage. Like a full set of armor, sex is offense *and* defense.

Sex acts to unite the two of you offensively and proactively through the release of the pleasure and bonding hormones referenced above. It deepens feelings of belonging and affection. In addition to those benefits, there are other ways physical touch strengthens your bodies and your marriage: "Touch activates the [vagus nerve and the] brain's orbitofrontal cortex, which [are] linked to feelings of reward and compassion." A warm touch signals safety and trust and "calms cardiovascular stress," and when you touch each other (even nonsexually), oxytocin levels increase, which inhibits the brain's fear center.[6]

> Sex in marriage keeps the two of you facing each other rather than looking elsewhere for intimacy, belonging, and comfort.

Sex is also defense. It is a shield against the attacks Satan is leveling against your marriage every day.

One author refers to sex as "a spiritual battleground."[7] And so it is. Whether our struggle is with discontentment, lust, resentment, apathy, or the perversion of a good gift, sexuality is a part of us that is rife with danger and vulnerable to attack.

---

6. Dacher Keltner, "Hands On Research: The Science of Touch," *Greater Good* Magazine, September 29, 2010, https://greatergood.berkeley.edu/article/item/hands_on_research.
7. Juli Slattery, "Rethinking Sexuality in Your Life," *Java with Juli* podcast, July 16, 2018.

Sex in marriage is one way that God keeps you close and facing your spouse rather than looking elsewhere for intimacy, belonging, and comfort. God knows we are weak without the armor He has provided. He tells us in 1 Corinthians 7:5: "Do not deprive one another, except perhaps by agreement for a limited time, that you may devote yourselves to prayer; but then come together again so that Satan may not tempt you because of your lack of self-control."

This is why couples that neglect the sexual relationship often end in devastating fashion. Perhaps the marriage was naked because the spouses weren't.

So don't rush out onto the battlefield—the workplace, other relationships, and the cultural barrage of bad ideas about bodies and sex—without protection. Strive together to deepen your connection through sex and to grow in bringing each other pleasure. Have tender, passionate, mutually delightful sex with your spouse and use the powerful armor God has given you for the protection of your marriage.

SEX IS DELIGHTFUL

Think about this: God didn't have to create colors, music, or tastebuds. He didn't have to create an astounding variety of flowers, birds, fish, trees, soil, insects, and every other facet of nature. Yet He did.

God didn't have to create our bodies in such a way that they fit together in astounding intimacy. He didn't have to create thousands of unique sensory receptors called "genital end bulbs" in the female clitoris and the head of the male penis to bring us exquisite pleasure during sex.[8] God didn't have to create the incredible interplay of body and brain that is an orgasm. Yet He did.

Our God is wildly creative, and His creativity is on full display in the act of sex. God could have made the sexual union strictly for procreation, yet He designed it to be so much more. He designed it to bring us great pleasure, to bond us together in a way that positively impacts every other area of our marriage. Sex is proof positive that God delights to delight His children with good gifts.

When you are sexually intimate with your spouse, you can rightly imagine that God is as pleased as any parent whose child plays with a new swing set with exhilaration and abandon. Your engaging in and enjoying sex is an act of gratitude to the Creator of your spouse and sex. Gifts are meant to be received with gladness. Nothing beautiful and exciting was designed to be shelved or neglected.

But what if sex doesn't feel beautiful and exciting?

Perhaps that's because it doesn't really please you, or it tends to happen the same way every time, or it doesn't tend to happen at all.

Have an open conversation with your spouse as to whether sex is a blessing to both of you. Make sure that both spouses' enjoyment and pleasure are prioritized. Regularly ask yourself: *Am I considering the interests of my spouse above my own?*

And if you both agree that sex isn't happening enough, make a plan to change that.

Yes, make a plan. Put it on the calendar if you must. This

---

8. Ross Pomeroy, "Six Fascinating Facts About Sexual Touch," *Real Clear Science* (blog), May 6, 2015, https://www.realclearscience.com/blog/2015/05/six_surprising_facts_about_sexual_touch.html.

doesn't sound very sexy, but trust us, scheduling sex can actually help with desire. This has been true in our marriage and for several couples we've counseled. Sex begins in the mind, and it's fun to look forward to it. Relieve yourselves of undue pressure. Not every encounter is going to be a long, sweaty, amazing experience. That's just not reality. Long encounters are great, but short ones can really keep the two of you connected.

If you feel like you've fallen into a sexual rut, you can make a plan to change that too. You can take turns in the driver's seat, where one spouse gets to decide how and when things happen. This is a great way to discover what your spouse enjoys most. Obviously, you wouldn't need to designate a "driver" every time, but it's one way to make sure sex remains a mutually pleasurable gift.

This will require consideration and kindness; no spouse should feel pressured to do something they find distasteful or uncomfortable. However, when both spouses come to the marriage bed seeking to put the other first, there is license to love each other in fun, new ways.

Above all, keep communication lines open about what each of you needs and enjoys. You may need to push through some initial awkwardness but talk about it anyway. If you do, talking about it will get easier and easier.

We started by reading a Christian book on sex together. This made talking about it so much less intimidating. You've got to walk softly when talking about sex, and a book gives you things to discuss without putting either of you on the defensive.[9] When

---

9. Do remember, though, not every Christian book on sex is a good one. Some authors we recommend in the area of sexual intimacy are Dr. Juli Slattery and Linda Dillow.

you do talk about it, your approach should be to encourage and affirm. Never use guilt or pressure. That is selfish immaturity and will most assuredly backfire on you. Your spouse will dread sex, rather than want it more.

Share your desires with each other, openly, but carefully. Never push your spouse to a place where they are not okay going. God has given us great beauty and freedom in sex, but He calls each of you to love the other more than yourself. Freedom in sex only extends to the point both of you are comfortable and feel loved.

Above all, keep talking about it, and keep pursuing a vibrant sex life.[10] Think of it as sharpening a skill you can use and enjoy the rest of your life. It's common sense, but we often treat sex differently for some reason. No team in any sport gets better by *wishing* they were better. They need to get out on the field, work together to grow as a team, and practice.

So, get out there and enjoy your practice! Nothing needs to be perfect. Just keep showing up.

We wish we had sought to grow in our physical relationship earlier in our marriage. There is no condemnation in Christ for being wherever you are, but we encourage you to strive for growth. You have nothing to lose, and so much sweetness to gain.

YOUR BIGGEST ACT OF GRACE

Even with all its pleasures and benefits, sex requires a lot of grace. Sex can be a struggle. It can be challenging to align libidos and schedules, not to mention the loss of desire for

---

10. For some, there may be roadblocks to enjoyment that a professional will need to address. If you are stuck, seek a licensed Christian counselor with experience in this area.

intimacy when you're having one of those days—or weeks—when you don't really like each other.

For some, grace-driven sex may look like choosing to serve your spouse in agreeing to (or even initiating) sex when you're honestly not in the mood. For others, it may look like denying yourself when you strongly desire sex, but your spouse doesn't. And for all of us, placing our sex lives under grace means *considering the interests of our spouse above our own.*

Sex should be more than a reward for good behavior, and more than a one-way, please-me street. When your marriage is under grace, you offer your spouse physical pleasure as a gift, not as a "good spouse" trophy. Likewise, you don't act selfishly and expect your spouse to give you sex whenever you want it.

When our spouse is struggling (and perhaps especially if they have sinned against us), offering sex can be one of the most powerful ways to display selfless love. On the other hand, giving up your desire for sex when your spouse is struggling physically or emotionally can be the right and loving thing to do. Again, it comes down to your willingness to put your spouse's interests ahead of your own.

Trust us, building your sex life on the foundation of grace can transform it. If both of you are relentlessly pursuing grace and applying grace to your sex life, your marriage—and sex—can be better than you ever hoped it would be.

One time Marilyn and I were in a bad place. We had been frustrated with each other for a while and weren't getting along. One evening, out of the blue, Marilyn started pursuing me sexually. I was like, *What are you doing?*

She said, "I love you and our marriage too much to allow distance to set in."

When you keep pursuing each other sexually whether you are both doing well or not, sin will lose its power to drive you apart. You'll stay close despite the ups and downs. (You may even find that the times you need to have sex the most are when you like each other the least.)

Again, most of what we've said in this chapter is referring to normal, day-to-day struggles in marriage. Nothing in this chapter is meant to imply that a spouse who is being emotionally or physically abused should feel compelled to pursue sex with the offender. And to be clear, we consider a pattern of manipulative, controlling behavior to be emotional abuse. The spouse who is struggling with a history of abuse or mistreatment needs help and forbearance here too. It is not the aim of this book to address the complex issues of couples in crisis. We seek to encourage couples who may struggle in some way with sex, yet their struggles are surmountable with open communication and the application of grace we discuss here.

When your sex life is under grace, sex is a marriage investment by a husband and wife who are mindful of God's design for sex, with all its protective, bonding, pleasurable powers. Sex is an extravagant act of love that is offered freely and joyfully. And that is sex that is a beautiful picture of the gospel.

DIGGING IN TO GRACE + INTENTIONALITY

A good sex life involves both spouses enjoying the benefits. How can you work with your spouse to make sure sex is mutually pleasurable to the fullest extent possible?

How can you be selfless and extend your spouse more grace in this area? How can you consider the interests of your spouse above your own?

What are you grateful for about your spouse in the area of sex?

1.

2.

3.

4.

5.

What ideas to invigorate your sex life do you want to discuss with your spouse?

1.

2.

3.

4.

5.

Grace and Money

Like sex, money can be a huge blessing or a huge stressor in marriage. When it's good, it's great, and when it's bad, it can destroy.

When Marilyn and I got married, we couldn't even talk about money without getting into an argument. Whenever the subject came up, I got stressed about our spending, and Marilyn felt judged. She'd express a desire to buy something for the house, and I'd say something like, "Wouldn't it be wiser to give that money to the church's adoption fund?" To her, everything I said felt like sideways preaching—probably because it was. We didn't communicate well, and we both pushed our own agenda.

Our experience is hardly uncommon. Money touches on so many basic themes: power, comfort, control, security, provision, beauty, and even survival. Spouses can each be convinced that their way is best, so there's plenty of room for disagreement. The stakes feel high. Emotions tend to run deep and hot. Ramsey Solutions, a financial education company founded by financial specialist and author Dave Ramsey, conducted a study that found disagreements over money are the second leading cause of divorce in America, only behind infidelity.[1]

Money matters in marriage are so difficult because two (sometimes very different) people have become one. It's a welding process, and welding involves intense heat and lots of sparks.

Dying to self can *really* feel like dying when it comes to how we spend our money. If you and your spouse frequently argue over finances, we want to encourage you. There is hope. Money can be an area of peace and synergy in your marriage as you grow in respecting each other, loving each other, honoring God, and using your money wisely.

MONEY TALKS

The path to financial hope starts with communication, both with your spouse and with the Lord.

God is faithful, and He didn't leave us where we began, in perpetual touchiness and disagreement over finances. Rather, He helped us discover keys to understanding and talking to each other about money.

Study

If you and your spouse are struggling to get on the same page over finances, you need to find out where each of you is coming from. This can be a low-pressure date night conversation, and it's something you should talk about sooner rather than later.

---

1. Ramsey Solutions, "Money Ruining Marriages in America," February 6, 2018, https://www.ramsey solutions.com/company/newsroom/releases/money-ruining-marriages-in-america.

The two biggest factors we've observed in counseling couples in this area are: differences in family of origin and differences in personality. These factors have sculpted you and your spouse into the spenders and savers that you are today. You need to understand them to be able to see why you each do the things you do.

Family of Origin

We weren't kidding about the date night thing, by the way. Go out to dinner and take turns answering the following questions:

How was money viewed or talked about in your family? Was money plentiful or scarce?

How was money used? Did your family tithe, save, make wise investments?

Was your family anti-debt? Would they readily borrow money for a purchase? Were things like credit cards a problem?

Did you save for things as a family?

Was eating out a common experience, or only for special occasions?

Was one person in charge of the family finances, or was it a team effort?

Was there healthy communication about money? Did your parents teach you wise ways of managing money? Was the topic taboo? Did it tend to cause arguments?

To your knowledge, was either parent deceptive about their purchases?

If money was tight for you but plentiful for your spouse, you probably have very different views on how to spend money. If you saw your parents argue over money, chances are that talking about finances makes you tense because you tend to think it will lead to an argument.

Ask yourself: How was I influenced by my family of origin as it relates to finances? How has that influenced my perspectives on spending? On saving? On giving?

Most likely, there were things about the way each of you was raised that you'd like to replicate. There are probably things you want to do differently too. Talk about these things together and discuss how you want *your* family to handle money.

When you know where each of you is coming from, you gain empathy and insight into where you can complement each other. When you pinpoint where and how you're seeing things differently, you can get on the same page much sooner.

Differences in Personality

Personality also plays a big part in how you view money.

Free-spirited people are often bigger spenders. They don't over-think things and can make purchases (even big ones) quickly. Sometimes extroverted, lively personalities can be generous with others, and perhaps too generous toward themselves.

Others have more methodical, analytical personalities. It may take days or weeks of processing to find any comfort with a financial decision. This can be a blessing for marriage or can be a significant source of conflict.

The way to marital harmony, no matter what kind of personality mash-up your marriage has, involves both self-awareness and learning about your spouse. Just like the family-of-origin influence, understanding your unique personalities—how they are similar and how they are different—will help you head in the same direction.

Early in our marriage, Brad and I realized we had a real problem because we can *both* be pretty free-spirited.

There was one day when I went to look at a house that was for sale at auction and called Brad to say I really liked it. He told me, "If you like it and think it's a good deal, just go with it!" I told him I was going to put an offer on it, and he was fine with that. He came home from work that day not knowing if we had bought a new house or not! Pretty dumb on both our parts.

By God's grace, we didn't get the house.

If you are both free spirits, you need outside accountability and structured boundaries. You should consider setting limits on what qualifies to be a "spur-of-the-moment" purchase. In our case, we've assimilated a group of people we respect. We don't make a major purchase without their input. This has been a huge blessing and protection for us.

If you both tend to be tighter with money, you may need accountability from someone you trust to ensure you are giving to the Lord, each other, and others generously, not putting your trust in possessions, and that you're enjoying God's good gifts instead of hoarding them.

As with the families of origin questions, it's a good idea to have a conversation where you share what you see in each other:

How does my personality impact our spending, giving, and saving?

Are our personality differences a regular source of conflict? If so, what do you wish I understood about the way you want to use money?

How do our differences help our marriage be more balanced? How are we a better team because we don't always see eye to eye? (By the way, this is a great point of conversation to have around other issues on which you differ, too—like communication tendencies, personalities, parenting, and so on.)

Be intentional in studying yourself and your spouse and what each of you brings to the *marriage-plus-money* equation. Be gracious as you seek to understand each other. Most importantly, listen.

Listen

One Saturday morning, Marilyn and I went to a big box home improvement store together (the blue one, not the orange one). At the time, we lived in a fixer-upper. Well, Marilyn saw it that way. Other than adding a basketball goal to the driveway, I didn't see the need for any changes.

I made the mistake of asking her, "If money wasn't an issue, what would you do to the house?"

She said, "Do you really want to know?"

"Sure."

Turns out, I should have asked if there was anything she *didn't* want to change about the house. Her eyes shone brightly as she pointed to something in nearly every aisle. "I would get one of these and two of those for our bedroom, and this for the kitchen. I'd install this, and change out that for this, and . . ."

She just kept going and going. My stomach dropped, and I got tenser and tenser. *There's no end in sight!* I said to myself. *I'll spend the rest of my life buying stuff I don't want or need.*

Marilyn was enjoying dreaming. I was envisioning a painful future and slipping into a bad mood. But the real problem was that I simply wasn't listening well. Marilyn wasn't wanting to stretch the budget or spend unwisely. She was just answering my question honestly: "What would you do if money was no object?"

What we should strive for in our marriages is an atmosphere where both spouses can share visions and desires—what to spend and how to spend it, what should be saved, how to invest—with absolute safety and comfort.

Money can be a shared resource used for provision, joy, and the glory of God. If we will listen and seek to understand before we start preaching or complaining, each of us can be heard. And it's remarkable how feeling understood disarms us.

Remember that timing can make all the difference. To keep conversations about finances from becoming combustible, we encourage you to have these conversations in a low-pressure setting. Don't wait to talk about money until right after you've paid the credit card bill (we've tried this) or when you're stressed out (tried this too). Make a date of it, be upfront and intentional, and take turns sharing and listening as you seek to get on the same page.

Examine Yourself

Finally, we need to remember that each of us has blind spots. And marriage often *reveals* our issues more than it *creates* new ones.

God has a lot to say about money in the Bible. God cares deeply about the way we use and think about money. Because of its unique intimacy, marriage has a way of exposing whether our view of money lines up with what the Bible teaches. God can use marriage to help us see whether our hearts are fully submitted to Him in this area or are bent toward the god of money.

When you get married:

insecurities about money are exposed to your spouse;

greed or frugality is easy for a spouse to see in the way you have been managing your finances;

poor stewardship or debt is no longer able to be hidden;

selfishness rises to the surface when you have to spend what used to be "your" money on the necessities of the household.

Before we got married, I could spend what I wanted. When I went to buy an engagement ring, I checked how much money I had in my account, and that was how much I spent. No emergency fund. Nobody to question me. However, when I got married, my lack of wisdom and my selfishness were put on display.

Marriage changes the money game in a lot of uncomfortable ways. This is an act of God's grace toward us as He grows us up into spiritual maturity. God uses marriage—and sometimes our spouse, specifically—as an avenue of grace to grow us more into His likeness.

So don't resent your spouse for the ways they challenge you about how you view and use money. They are a tool of sanctification, and finances is just one area where most of us could use some refining.

PERSPECTIVE CHECK

Hang on a minute. We just said marriage exposes whether our view of money lines up with Scripture—but do we know what Scripture actually says about money? If we get that wrong, we're going to have vertical *and* horizontal problems in our marriage. So, let's take a crash course in the theology of money.

It's Not Ours

First, when we talk about the ways we use our money, we need to understand that it's not really *our* money, it is God's. Everything we have is from Him.

The earth is the LORD's and the fullness thereof, the world and those who dwell therein.[2]

[The LORD said] "Who has first given to me, that I should repay him? Whatever is under the whole heaven is mine."[3]

Sometimes we can be tempted to think that we've worked hard, earned, and own the money in our bank accounts. But Scripture is clear that God lays claim to everything under the sun. All our riches are gifts from Him. All our possessions should be considered "on loan."

As the parable of the talents makes clear,[4] we are to steward well the money God has entrusted to us. We steward it well precisely because it's not our money; it belongs to the King.

If we are rich, our wealth should not cause us to become proud. An abundance of riches should lead us to worship the

---

2. Psalm 24:1.
3. Job 41:11.
4. See Matthew 25:14–30.

Giver who has so generously blessed us. We should seek to steward God's money wisely and use it for His purposes. If we are poor, our need for money should point us to our great Provider. In Jesus, we've been given all we ever truly *need*: "And this same God who takes care of me will supply all your needs from his glorious riches, which have been given to us in Christ Jesus."[5] A lack of money shouldn't be considered a curse because money can bring with it a heap of trouble.

It Is Dangerous

The second thing Scripture makes clear is that the love of money is dangerous for the human soul.

"No servant can serve two masters, for either he will hate the one and love the other, or he will be devoted to the one and despise the other. You cannot serve God and money."[6]

But those who desire to be rich fall into temptation, into a snare, into many senseless and harmful desires that plunge people into ruin and destruction. For the love of money is a root of all kinds of evils. It is through this craving that some have wandered away from the faith and pierced themselves with many pangs.[7]

The pursuit of wealth is a slippery slope. When we are working to gain more and more money, temptations to compromise often increase—whether as ethical issues like dishonesty or something closer to home like shorting time with our families. There's nothing wrong with being rich. But there is *everything*

---

5. Philippians 4:19 NLT.
6. Luke 16:13.
7. 1 Timothy 6:9–10.

wrong with idolatry, greed, vanity, covetousness, pride, and forsaking our kingdom calling. Having money makes those kinds of sins easier to fall into.

No matter our financial situation, it is important that we regularly submit our desires to God.

Search your heart and ask God to search it too. The love of money is so insidious that we must always be on guard, as Jesus encourages us: "Take care, and be on your guard against all covetousness, for one's life does not consist in the abundance of his possessions."[8]

It Is a Gift to Be Given Away

Our money is on loan from the Owner of all things, and clutching it too tightly is bad for our souls. This leads us to our last point: Money should be given away.

God does not bless us so we can hoard piles of wealth. God's generosity toward us is meant to inspire us to be generous with others.

In 2 Corinthians, where Paul encourages the Corinthian church to give to the church in Jerusalem, he reminds them that God supplies the grace to give, and that God Himself gives to us freely and abundantly. This should cause us to glorify our gracious God, and to be "rich" toward others.

"You will be enriched in every way to be generous in every way, which through us will produce thanksgiving to God."[9]

God alone is our hope, and life in Him is the only true life. When we start to grasp this truth, it loosens our grip on material things. We don't need extravagance or the admiration of

---

8. Luke 12:15.
9. 2 Corinthians 9:11.

others when we have an eternity in glory secure in our future. Ask yourself, *Where do I need to confess wrong thinking about money to God and to my spouse? Is there a way that my wrong perspective has caused division instead of unity?*

IT'S ALL ABOUT ~~THE BENJAMINS~~ GRACE

Understanding our spouse's perspective and knowing what God says is fundamental to navigating money talks in marriage. It's important that we get those right. But theory must become practice. Let's talk about how a mindset of grasping God's grace toward us and extending it to our spouse plays out in four ways related to money: spending, saving, giving, and debt.

Spending

Matthew 6:21 states, "For where your treasure is, there your heart will be also." This truth applies to *all* areas of life, but it seems most obvious when we look at where we are spending our money. To quote Dave Ramsey, "The flow of money in a family represents the value system under which that family operates."[10]

When looking at your marriage, you need an objective way to determine your values. This is where the strategy of "money monitoring" comes in. Money monitoring is like budgeting, but different in a few key ways.

The typical approach to budgeting goes something like this: set parameters for every spending category in your lives, grit your teeth while trying to stick to it, point out your spouse's

---

10. Dave Ramsey, *Financial Peace* (New York: Viking, 1997), 183.

spending patterns with a sharp eye, and sooner or later chuck it all in frustration.

Money monitoring is different because the two of you will watch where your money goes and make changes accordingly. It's a grace-based, teamwork approach to making sure your spending habits line up with your family values.

One speaker suggested three steps to monitor your spending together:[11]

First, document your spending for two months. This means every receipt gets recorded into a category.

Next, sit down and look at it together, remembering grace, of course.

Then, adjust if necessary. Decide together which categories need to be trimmed and which need more resources allocated their way.

When we keep track of where we are spending money, we are less likely to fight about it. We can both see it there, in black and white, without feeling our spouse is exaggerating or being unfair. If one category consistently passes the limits the two of you have decided on, there is room for discussion on whether some money should be moved around or not.

There is no "You blew the budget!" There is only "What do we need to change?"

As for larger purchases, we have found great freedom in what we call the "2–0 Rule"—if we don't *both* agree on the purchase, we don't buy it. (You can decide together what your

---

11. Andy Stanley, Money Talks series, sermon "Keep Track," from North Point Community Church, Alpharetta, GA, February 25, 2019.

minimum price point is for this kind of purchase.) It's important to consider your spouse above yourself, though, so this doesn't become a formula for control. Remember, God charges us to consider others above ourselves.[12]

Clearly, we need to be wise. We shouldn't be spending money frivolously just because our spouse wants us to. But often it seems that the spouse who tends to be tighter with money may use "wisdom" as an excuse not to bless their husband or wife, and this lends itself to regular conflict. The spender spouse has desires the saver may not understand, and it's easy for the latter to wave these off as unnecessary, or even foolish. Constantly being told no, the spender retreats into resentment or hidden rebellion.

This scenario is something Marilyn and I have seen frequently.

When I practiced law, I had a client ask for her settlement money in two separate checks. I was fine with it but asked her why. She said, "This is the check I am going to show my husband. This other one will be spending money for me!"

As a mentor once told me, "You should be more generous with your spouse than anyone else, including yourself." His challenge helped me realize I was tighter with Marilyn than I was with anyone else.

Do the work of getting on the same page regarding what "wisdom" looks like for your family. Then together adopt the motto that, "If it's wise and you want it, it's yours." Creating an atmosphere of "for-ness" instead of an atmosphere of "me vs. you" will keep your hearts open to each other.

In our case, when Marilyn felt like I was putting her first,

---

12. Philippians 2:3.

it swung wide the doors of communication in this area, and in others. When we feel like the other is for and not against us, we are free to voice our desires without fear. And when we know the other wants to bless us, it's easier to lay down our desires when they disagree with us.

Saving

We all know that saving is a wise thing to do. Proverbs 13:22 says, "A good man leaves an inheritance to his children's children." We also know that rainy days will come, and wise men and women are prepared for them. But what if you and your spouse disagree on how to save?

First, it's a good idea to talk about where those different opinions come from. (If you haven't caught on by now, we're big on knowledge and understanding to defuse conflict.) Outside of a heated moment, arrive together on a percentage or goal that you can agree is wise for your family to set aside.

Another aspect of your saving conversation should be talking about hopes and dreams. Dreaming together is wonderfully bonding, and a lot of fun. Share with each other where you'd like to be in five, ten, and twenty years. What goals can you save toward together? Big and small, what bucket-list items do you want to save for?

I (Marilyn) love to dream about owning a bed-and-breakfast, and how we could use it for marriage retreats. It may never happen, but it's good for our hearts to be open and share our dreams with each other.

Giving

You'll find an abundance of Scriptures that encourage us to give to others.

Each one must give as he has decided in his heart, not reluctantly or under compulsion, for God loves a cheerful giver.[13]

It is more blessed to give than to receive.[14]

A generous person will prosper; whoever refreshes others will be refreshed.[15]

I think the main reason God emphasizes giving so much is that it brings us into alignment with His character. God is an extravagant Giver. He wants us to resemble Him more and more as we "excel in this grace of giving."[16]

How do you decide what or who to give to and how much?

For us, we give first to our local church, and then discuss ministries the Lord has put on our hearts. As for figures for these ministries, we pray about it separately, arrive at a number in our head, then come together and compare. It's uncanny how often our numbers are the same or extremely close. When they're not the same, we do our best to go with the higher number.

Another thing we do that makes giving a joy is to put money in the budget for what we call "fun giving." This fund goes toward surprising people with meals, giving large tips, and sending surprise gifts.

Blessing others through giving together is a sweet grace of God. It's so much fun to scheme together how to delight and

---

13. 2 Corinthians 9:7.
14. Acts 20:35.
15. Proverbs 11:25 NIV.
16. 2 Corinthians 8:7 NIV.

meet the needs of others. I'd encourage you to try to grow each year in how much you give.

Debt

In our experience working with married couples, debt is one of the heaviest weights that a marriage can carry. And it is certainly enough to tear you apart if you let it. So how do we mitigate it? How do we fight the "you deserve it" sales pitch we constantly hear from our culture?

We'll tell you the best financial advice we've ever received: If you can't pay cash for it, you can't afford it.[17] A mortgage is typically brought up as a possible exception to this rule. We agree that there's nothing wrong with a mortgage if you can put in enough of a down payment to avoid unnecessary costs and lower your monthly payment. But apart from that, try to do everything possible to live according to that philosophy.

A law school classmate of mine (Brad's) bought the nicest house he could afford after he graduated and began working, but whenever we invited him out to dinner or events, he always turned us down because he "didn't really have the money for it right now." It was sadly ironic that he had such a nice house he couldn't afford to leave it.

A cautionary tale, but this principle is true for all of us: When you aggressively avoid debt, you have more money to spend on things that matter. You have more to give, save, and spend on enjoying each other.

If you are working to be free from debt, do not feel stress or condemnation from this chapter. It is a noble goal you are working toward.

---

17. Thank you, Bill Barron!

As with all other financial areas we've discussed, work together to set goals and achieve them. Commit as a team that you're going to monitor your spending, save a certain amount for these purposes, have a blast giving, get out of debt, and then agree on the path that will get you there.

We pray money is an area of your marriage in which you can bless others, richly enjoy God's good gifts, and unite around the common goal of glorifying God with all He's given you.

DIGGING IN TO GRACE + INTENTIONALITY

In what area do you struggle the most related to finances?

Spending

Saving

Giving

Debt

Specifically, what action steps can you take to grow in good stewardship?

1.

2.

3.

4.

5.

How does your spouse benefit your family in the area of finances?

1.

2.

3.

4.

5.

How can you demonstrate grace and generosity toward your spouse regarding finances?

1.

2.

3.

4.

5.

Afterword

Grace + Intentionality = Growth + the Gospel

INTENTIONALITY IS THE KEY TO GROWTH

A businessman who came to a Grace Marriage session once told us, "I have a growth mentality in business. I'm always looking for ways to improve, analyzing what could be done better, and asking myself what the next step should be. I'm going to start applying that same concept to my marriage. My marriage goal used to be, *Stay married 'til death do us part.* My new goal is, *Enjoy my wife more and more every year!*"

This guy gets it.

Persistently seeking growth makes it hard to stagnate. When each of us takes ownership for bringing life, creativity, and zeal to our marriage, our relationship becomes more lively, fun, and passionate. Instead of waiting for our spouse to morph into the

199

ideal mate, we can work toward being the most gracious and intentional spouse we can be.

But after exploring what it could look like to grow in grace and intentionality in all aspects of life—from your bedroom to your bank account—do you know where to start?

We encourage you to remember Jesus' words in Matthew 6:21: "Where your treasure is, there your heart will be also," and Paul's exhortation in 2 Corinthians 9:6: "Whoever sows sparingly will also reap sparingly, and whoever sows bountifully will also reap bountifully." A consistent, ongoing rhythm of investing in your marriage will be necessary if you want it to thrive. Your resources of money, creativity, and time must be sown—bountifully and regularly—if it is going to bear fruit.

Doing things like dating your spouse, intentionally seeking connection with them, and retreating away together regularly will keep you moving forward together. Put in the big efforts and the little ones. Never underestimate the importance of prioritizing each other in everyday life.

A lot of spouses and even many churches seem to be permanently set on reactive mode; marriages only get attention when there's a problem. But we don't dump a gallon of water on a potted plant and then expect it to blossom and bloom all year long. Your car won't deliver peak performance if you only change the oil every hundred thousand miles. Everything that needs care needs *consistent* care to flourish. We invest in our marriages . . . and then we keep on investing.

We've got to change the way we think about marriage. "Good enough" can't be good enough. Being just "okay" is not okay.

Marriage can be so much more than a utilitarian partnership

or a stable arrangement in which we do a nice job of tolerating each other. If God designed marriage as a witness to the love between Christ and the church, then it should be a union of astounding, magnetic, sacrificial love. In fact, apart from your union with Christ, marriage should be the relationship that you pursue most passionately—to grow in serving, blessing, knowing, loving, and in true intimacy.

We have found that, without a structure and a plan, growth rarely occurs. As John Maxwell says, "Change is inevitable. Growth is optional."[1] We are asking you to choose growth. If you're looking for a practical place to start, we invite you to visit gracemarriage.com and get on a pathway of ongoing investment and growth in your marriage.

GRACE IS THE GOSPEL

It has always been our aim to promote grace between spouses because we've tasted and seen the difference it makes, both for us and for others we've counseled.

But this book is primarily about the love and grace of God.

Grace is the message of the gospel. It is by and through God's grace we are saved. It is by and through God's grace that we extend grace to one another.

God's grace is the inspiration for our grace. Our grace for each other is an outpouring of gratitude and obedience to the One who loved us so much He did not spare His own Son. When we grasp how much we are loved, our hearts are stirred

1. John Maxwell, "I do know this about growth," Facebook, June 19, 2013, https://www.facebook.com/ JohnCMaxwell/photos/i-do-know-this-about-growth-change-is-inevitable-growth-is-optional-to- grow-you-/10151620381877954/.

to love much in return. We can delight in one another because our Father in heaven delights in us.

God's grace is the headwater of our grace. His river of mercy flows rich and deep, a source of refreshment for our souls that will never run dry. Receiving His grace empowers us to give it away to those around us. And when we walk in grace, daily receiving and extending it, amazing things can happen.

We have more fun together. We seek to bless and find ourselves blessed. We seek to infuse creativity and intentionality into our marriages and find ourselves reaping a harvest of joy, affection, and connection.

We grow in godliness. Sin has no dominion over our marriages as we keep little things little, move toward each other when we struggle, and become servants of reconciliation for each other. We are freed from condemnation to love God and love each other better.

We find that this rhythm of receiving and extending grace has become the new norm, and that the old performance mindset doesn't fit as well as it used to.

We abide in Christ and find that the One who always keeps His promises surely delivers for us. Rooted in His grace, our marriages bear much fruit . . . to our great delight, and to the praise of God's glory.

Acknowledgments

From Brad and Marilyn:

This book, from the concepts within to the moment of its publishing, has been a team effort by many who have instructed, encouraged, come alongside, served, and championed us. We owe a great debt of thanks to the following persons (and more).

To the Grace Marriage Team: Thank you to the most amazing group of people we could ever hope to work with. Your wisdom, encouragement, and knack for having fun make our lives and this book what it is today. Jeremy Bennett, thank you for taking a courageous leap of faith to do marriage ministry with us. Brittany Cragg, it is a privilege to work with someone so talented, wise, and theologically sound.

To Moody Publishers: Thank you for being gospel partners. Every step of publishing this book with you has been encouraging to our souls. Your combination of grace, wisdom, and excellence is remarkable.

To Debra Fileta, Sheila Wray Gregoire, Juli Slattery, and Gary Thomas: Thank you for influencing our teaching on married sex. Special thanks to Juli and Sheila for your input on the content of chapter 11; your thoughtful counsel greatly benefited the chapter.

To Jerry and Judy Rhoads (Brad's parents): Thank you for modeling a lasting marriage. Thank you for supporting us in everything we have ever done. We could not feel more loved.

To Ruth Hudson (Marilyn's mom): Thank you for modeling a beautiful marriage that put flesh and bones on "till death do us part." Thank you for your ongoing support in life and ministry. And to Larson Hudson (Marilyn's dad): We miss you every day of our lives. I, Brad, thank you for loving my wife so well; what a gift that was to me. I, Marilyn, thank you for being the most wonderful father a girl could ever have. You adored and delighted in me my entire life.

To the Grace Marriage board—Brian Crall, Lori Grizzell, Jon Gibson, and the late Doug Hignell: Thank you for guiding us, loving us, and supporting us in our lives and ministry. Each of you is truly a gift from God, and we thank Him for you all the time. Grace Marriage and this book would not exist but for your ongoing care. Doug taught us what it looked like to live a life of receiving and extending grace. We can say with near certainty that the ministry of Grace Marriage would not exist but for God's work through Doug. And just as Doug taught me (Brad) how to live, he showed me how to die. As he was dying from brain cancer, Doug was as much at peace as he was when he was healthy and at the helm of a large corporation. His hope truly was not in this world, and now he is enjoying his eternal reward.

To our children—Madeline, Kate, Abby, Matthew, and Rachel: Thank you for loving us and teaching us to love. You are the absolute coolest kids ever, and you make life one fun, crazy ride. We love spending time with you.

To Dr. Juli Slattery: Thank you for your phenomenal encouragement in ministry, and more so, your perpetual encouragement to pursue Christ. God's work through you has been an invaluable gift to Grace Marriage.

To Chris Rhoads: Thank you for being the best law partner, brother, and friend. I (Brad) enjoyed practicing law with you and thank God for your ongoing support.

To Tom and Elizabeth Rhoads: Thank you for pursuing us; you were truly used by God to change the course of our marriage.

To Bill and Jo Barron: Thank you for investing in us. Walking with you over the years, both in life and in ministry, has been a gift we treasure greatly.

To Jamus Edwards and Pleasant Valley Community Church: Thank you for being supportive, valuing marriage, praying for us, and being a huge part of the change that is occurring in thousands of marriages.

And finally, to all the many precious friends and relatives too numerous to name here: You are a gift straight from God. Your generosity with time and resources humbles us and points us to Jesus. Thank you for the many ways you have supported us and shared with us your love and wisdom.

From Brittany:

To Mark Cragg, my champion, companion, and the love of my life: Marriage to you has been the crucible in which so much of my sanctification has been forged; thank you for being a willing vessel of God's pursuit of and gracious love toward me. Thank you for always bringing me back to Jesus in your love, admonishment, and encouragement. Thank you for your tireless cheer and patience as I spent so many precious evening hours writing and editing for this project. If I know anything about choosing grace, it's because I've learned it with you. I love you.

To Jack and Kathy Tarr, and to John and Kay Cragg: Finding two people whose parents not only remain married, but still love, serve, and deeply enjoy each other is hard to do. Mark and I are blessed beyond measure to be such a couple—the gift we've been given in your faithfulness to the Lord and to each other is not lost on us. Thank you.

To Brad and Marilyn: Thank you for your shining example of grace in action—you two are the real deal and truly an inspiration. It's no overstatement to say writing this book with you has changed my life.

To Tim Grissom and Pam Pugh: Thank you for lending your significant editing prowess to the many stages of this book. Your insights and incisions were a gift.

FOR CHURCHES · FOR BUSINESS · FOR COUPLES

Marriage ministry
reimagined.

ASSESS + ENGAGE + GROW

An ongoing path and plan toward healthy, Christ-centered marriages.

We help churches reimagine marriage ministry and equip husbands and wives to build marriages that reflect the Gospel.

GraceMarriage.com